At Issue

| Transportation
| Infrastructure

Other Books in the At Issue Series:

At Issue

Transportation Infrastructure

Noah Berlatsky, Book Editor

GREENHAVEN PRESS
A part of Gale, Cengage Learning

GALE
CENGAGE Learning·

Detroit • New York • San Francisco • New Haven, Conn • Waterville, Maine • London

Elizabeth Des Chenes, *Director, Publishing Solutions*

© 2012 Greenhaven Press, a part of Gale, Cengage Learning.

Gale and Greenhaven Press are registered trademarks used herein under license.

For more information, contact:
Greenhaven Press
27500 Drake Rd.
Farmington Hills, MI 48331-3535
Or you can visit our Internet site at gale.cengage.com

For product information and technology assistance, contact us at

Gale Customer Support, 1-800-877-4253
For permission to use material from this text or product, submit all requests online at www.cengage.com/permissions

Further permissions questions can be e-mailed to permissionrequest@cengage.com

Articles in Greenhaven Press anthologies are often edited for length to meet page requirements. In addition, original titles of these works are changed to clearly present the main thesis and to explicitly indicate the author's opinion. Every effort is made to ensure that Greenhaven Press accurately reflects the original intent of the authors. Every effort has been made to trace the owners of copyrighted material.

Cover image © Images.com/Corbis.

LIBRARY OF CONGRESS CATALOGING-IN-PUBLICATION DATA

Transportation infrastructure / Noah Berlatsky, book editor.
    p. cm. -- (At issue)
    ISBN 978-0-7377-6541-0 (hardcover) -- ISBN 978-0-7377-6542-7 (pbk.)
    1. Transportation--United States--Finance. 2. Transportation--United States--Planning. 3. Infrastructure (Economics)--United States. I. Berlatsky, Noah.
    HE206.2.T7152 2012
    388.0973--dc23
                                                         2012016203

Printed in the United States of America
1 2 3 4 5 6 7 16 15 14 13 12

HE
206.2
715Q
2012

Contents

Introduction

Bicycles, like cars, require infrastructure investment. Bicyclists need bike lanes, and they need street designs that make it safe to ride bicycles around cars.

Many people argue that the federal government should spend more money on bicycle infrastructure. For example, Darren Flusche, a policy analyst for the League of American Bicyclists, argues in a 2009 report that investing in bicycling infrastructure can have substantial benefits for the economy. Flusche points to Maine, which has widened road shoulders and created shared-use bike paths, and partially as a result generates $66 million a year in bicycle tourism. He also points to North Carolina's Outer Banks, which, he says, "generates $60 million in economic activity through bicycle tourism. They spent $6.7 million on bicycle infrastructure and have seen an annual nine to one return on that one-time investment."

Flusche also argues that there is an underserved demand for bicycle infrastructure. He points to a 2002 National Transportation Safety Administration study, in which less than half of those surveyed were happy with the infrastructure their communities provided for bicycles. Flusche notes that "the most popular changes for bicyclists were additional bike lanes, paths, and trails, followed by improvements to existing facilities."

Ray LaHood, the US Secretary of Transportation, has also argued that government should invest in bike infrastructure. On January 13, 2011, at his official blog, LaHood cited a report showing that bike lanes and bike-friendly infrastructure create "more direct jobs, more indirect jobs, and more *induced* jobs per dollar" than roadwork. LaHood also pointed to a survey showing that 67 percent of the public would like cities to be designed to increase physical activity. LaHood concluded,

"Putting the two studies together creates a powerful argument for continuing the Department of Transportation's support for bicycle and pedestrian infrastructure projects."

Another often-cited benefit of creating bicycle-friendly cities is environmental. Will Cornwell, writing at the San Francisco Bicycle Coalition website, claims that, "Air pollution, global climate change, traffic congestion, economic dependance on fossil fuels are all reduced by biking instead of driving." He adds that "Californians avoid producing seven tons of smog-forming gases per day by getting on bikes."

Other commentators have been more skeptical of the value of spending public money on bicycle infrastructure. For example, Ocean State Policy Research Institute (OSPRI) in its *2011 Rhode Island Piglet Book*, which highlights unnecessary government spending, argued that the state wasted $4.8 million dollars when it paid for new bike paths and other bike infrastructure throughout the state.

Similarly, Randall O'Toole in a January 8, 2008, article for the *Los Angeles Times* contends that many bicycle infrastructure projects are wasteful and inefficient. He says that urban planners and those in government are often ideologically opposed to automobiles, and "the name of the game for them is to divert as many highway dollars to non-highway projects as possible." He adds that as a result, cities spend their highway money on "multimillion-dollar bicycle overpasses, exclusive bike paths and other expensive facilities." O'Toole argues that these projects are used by only few people and are therefore an inefficient way to spend funds. He suggests that, instead of creating dedicated bike lanes, cities should create bicycle boulevards—low-traffic streets near larger thoroughfares to which bicycle traffic can be directed. He also argues that bicyclists should pay a fee for every mile they cycle, which could be used to fund improved bicycle infrastructure.

Fawn Johnson at the *National Journal* explains in an October 11, 2011, post that Republicans in Congress dislike spending money on bike paths that they feel are needed for roads. This has become increasingly true as the federal budget has tightened so that even money for roads and bridges is under pressure. For example, Oklahoma Republican senator James M. Inhofe, the ranking member of the US Senate Committee on Environment and Public Works, has argued that bike paths and walkway improvements should not receive federal funds. At the most, Johnson says, Republicans maintain that federal funds should not be directly appropriated for bikes but should instead be given in block grants to states. States can then decide for themselves whether to spend the funds solely on roads or whether to set aside some money for bicycles.

The viewpoints in *At Issue: Transportation Infrastructure* will look at the various issues surrounding the government's funding of infrastructure projects, as well as the debate over whether these projects, including those for roads, bridges, and trains, are wise investments of public money.

1

A History of Infrastructure

Anthony R. Tomazinis

Anthony R. Tomazinis is professor emeritus of city and regional planning at the University of Pennsylvania School of Design.

Infrastructure has been an important consideration since the earliest human habitations. In the United States, the era of large-scale federal infrastructure investment began in the 1930s. Since then, the government has been closely involved in public works, including transportation, sewage systems, housing, and more. The largest public works investment in the history of the world is the US interstate highway system, constructed from the 1950s to the 1980s. The government has also invested heavily in public transit systems. The public has become increasingly concerned about the environmental impact of infrastructure investment, and about whether infrastructure investment should be funded publically or by private entities.

Human settlements started as simple places, where people could live with some level of convenience and enjoy some measure of security against outside threats. Although hunting, gathering, and fishing were the first preoccupations of primitive man, it was soon discovered that some kinds of tools had to be made for even these elementary activities. In addition, they soon found out that provisions should be made to help them face the adversities of the local weather and the

Anthony R. Tomazinis, "Infrastructure." *Dictionary of American History, 3rd ed.* Belmont, CA: The Gale Group, 2003, pp. 355–358. Copyright © 2003 by The Gale Group. All rights reserved. Reproduced by permission.

hostilities of other tribes and wild animals. These support facilities were the first elemental components of an urban infrastructure that made living, gathering, hunting, and producing possible.

Early Towns

All these old truths remain relevant to more recent human habitation experiences. The first "towns" of the Far West in the United States almost instinctively were formed where transport was available and where the provision of water was secure. Settlements that neglected to pay proper attention to these two primary components of the needed support systems, or failed to have an elemental concern and provision for drainage, usually experienced an early demise.

The "new era" of American infrastructure started in the Great Depression.

Concerns for additional support structures continued in most settlements soon after their establishment. A marketplace, some form of a city hall, a police station, and a courthouse tended to pop up soon in the life of a city. A school was added before long, as well as a clinic or doctor's office. In this way the first infrastructure services and facilities were included very early in the life of most urban developments.

Throughout history, infrastructure systems and services have continuously evolved in both technology and organization. Indeed, in many instances, social scientists measure the level of civilization or advancements of a society on the basis of the richness and articulation of the infrastructure systems that society has in place. Another way to gauge the importance of infrastructure is to note that all the progressive movements of the nineteenth and twentieth centuries have, in essence, focused on the need to improve one or another infrastructure system in meeting one or another social, humanitarian, or economic need. In the case of the American metropolis of the early twenty-first century, one can easily distinguish at least fifty systems and subsystems that constitute the city's infrastructure, ranging from large-scale transportation and water projects to neighborhood medical clinics and libraries.

Birth of Modern Infrastructure: The Great Depression

The "new era" of American infrastructure started in the Great Depression. In 1932 Americans elected a president [Franklin D. Roosevelt] and Congress that believed in an active role for the federal government in creating jobs for the multitude of unemployed Americans. Within the framework of a newly coined economic theory in macroeconomics by John Maynard Keynes [who argued that government spending could stimulate economic growth], the new president started with a modest list of infrastructure projects, such as federal administrative buildings. He soon extended the enterprise to railroad stations, post office buildings, irrigation projects, road repairing and expansion, hydroelectric dams, and even a regional multipurpose district of major proportions under the name of the Tennessee Valley Authority. Even in outlying areas, the Rural Electrification Administration extended another infrastructure system.

Following the example of the federal government, many states initiated plans for infrastructure systems in their territories. Notable among these are the projects carried out by Robert Moses in New York, city and state, who extended and improved the transportation and parks systems of the greater New York region by leaps and bounds, adding many miles of parkways, bridges, and tunnels. The new age of great urban public works was on.

The intervention of World War II interrupted this stream of initiatives throughout the country. But at the same time, additional infrastructure components were added as new airports, new towns, and new harbors appeared on the map as a result of the war effort.

By the time the [interstate highway system] program was completed . . . , the expenditures had reached about $111 billion, making it the largest single public works project in history.

Immediately after the war, government leaders worried about a potential new economic recession and, desiring to do something good for the returning millions of victorious war veterans, initiated a major housing assistance program. This action was followed by the 1947 Urban Renewal Act and then with the Housing Act of 1954, both of which placed all three levels of government in the midst of a new nationwide effort to plan and improve the service systems of all cities with more than 50,000 people.

In particular the 1954 act included section 701, which invited each of these cities to produce a community plan in which six of the seven central components were focused on transportation and the other infrastructure systems needed for the growth of the community. Once the plan was approved by local, state, and federal agencies, each community could apply for a major share of the cost of construction paid by the federal (and state) government. Since then, section 701 and its extensions have produced a multitude of local infrastructure improvements and expansions for most of the cities of the country.

The Interstate Highway System and Environmental Regulations

In 1956, Congress approved the Interstate Highway Act, proposed by President [Dwight] Eisenhower as both a national defense program in the midst of the Cold War (permitting large-scale military units' rapid movement from one part of the country to the other) and as an economic measure that would increase the efficiency of the American economy. The program initially proposed 41,000 miles of expressways criss-crossing the continental United States, with an initial overall budget not to exceed $41 billion. By 1962 the program was extended to about 42,500 miles and included not only the interstate expressways but also components for all major metropolitan areas of the country. The actual plans in each case included segments connecting the suburban areas with the central business districts of each region, crosstown expressways, and one or two beltways. By the time the whole program was completed in the late 1980s, the expenditures had reached about $111 billion, making it the largest single public works project in history, far exceeding the pyramids of Egypt, the Tennessee Valley Authority multipurpose program, and the federal hydroelectric and irrigation dams program of the western states.

The interstate expressway system has been a major force for change in urban America, influencing national location patterns of American industry and substantially increasing the productivity and efficiency of both the primary and secondary sectors of the economy. With regard to the residential patterns of American metropolitan areas, the expressway program of the 1960s, 1970s, and 1980s contributed to the changes and upheavals of that period. Many significant mistakes have been noted on specific, localized parts of the system, due frequently to administrative directives that were very constrictive and necessitated the elimination of whole neighborhoods and/or historical communities.

Another federal program that had a major impact on urban infrastructure systems is the one based on section 208 of the Clean Water Act of 1970. This program required that the sewage of all urban areas be cleaned before its emission into streams, rivers, and lakes. Federal assistance was in most cases up to 90 percent of the cost of each project. As a result of this program, the level of impurities in streams, rivers, and lakes in the United States improved dramatically. Primary sewage treatment became universal, removing about 65 percent of all impurities. Secondary and tertiary treatments were expanded on a scale that removed 90 to 95 percent of the impurities (and in some cases, up to 98 percent). By the end of the century, U.S. urban areas were disposing of effluent in streams, rivers, and lakes that was typically cleaner than the natural flow of their waters would produce.

The Clean Water Act also has assisted many cities in building whole new water and sewerage systems, as well as expanding and improving existing ones. In some cases improvements were essential, as in the case of Manhattan Island, where, for the first time, purification plants made it possible to discontinue the practice of releasing raw sewage into the Hudson River. The Clean Water Act and its amendments also mandated improvement of the effluents emitted by industries, commercial enterprises, and even major private residential construction sites. The National Environmental Protection Act of 1969 (NEPA) introduced sweeping measures for cleaning up the American natural environment, making the thirty years between 1970 and 2000 a historic period in the environmental and infrastructure history of the country and of the world.

The solid waste collection and disposal system was also radically improved between 1970 and 2000. Gone are the casual solid waste dumps at the outskirts of the cities, replaced by sanitary landfills. Almost gone, thanks to air pollution regulations, are the solid waste incinerators in some central parts of cities, built there to minimize the transport costs of collected waste. In their place are either electrolytic burners or sophisticated trash-to-energy installations where high-temperature burners generate electricity for local electric utilities. Solid waste collection and disposal has been improved with new trucks designed to carry compacted waste. Such trucks bring the waste to special stations where further compacting produces uniform, high-density cubes that are transported to far-away sanitary disposal sites and used as landfill in natural cavities, excavation sites, or abandoned surface-mining sites. On the other side of the spectrum, extensive recycling of paper, glass, plastics, and aluminum had in some cities reached the level of 30 percent of the total volume of municipal solid waste by the beginning of the twenty-first century, creating new markets for such materials and extending the useful life of the basic product.

Libraries, Hospitals, and Public Transit

Infrastructural improvements also include the extensive urban and rural library systems in operation today throughout the country, a far cry from the typical unitary central library of the past. Branch libraries in almost every neighborhood or community are a common practice, with computerized data systems that permit almost instant service and control of the operations. Similarly, most major U.S. cities have networks of community clinics, with readily available first-aid service backed up by additional ambulatory transport service and connections with major hospitals.

At the beginning of the twenty-first century almost all major urban regions were planning major new transit systems and extensions of older ones.

Improvements in urban transportation in the last half of the twentieth century took the form of new and expanded heavy and light rail systems, an improved bus service system, and a paratransit system serving special population groups and communities.

Six heavy rail systems were introduced (Washington, D.C., Atlanta, Baltimore, Miami, Los Angeles, and San Francisco) in addition to the four systems already in place since before

World War II (New York, Chicago, Philadelphia, and Boston). Ten light rail systems were introduced (Miami, Detroit, San Diego, Buffalo, Pittsburgh, Portland, Sacramento, Denver, Hoboken, and Camden-Trenton). Several systems also have undergone continuous expansion (San Francisco and Los Angeles, for example). In all cases the budget and the effort has been enormous. For example, the Washington Metropolitan Area Transit Authority took more than thirty-four years to complete its 103-mile system, which began in 1967 with a projected cost of $2.5 billion and concluded in 2001 with an actual cost of about $10 billion.

At the beginning of the twenty-first century almost all major urban regions were planning major new transit systems and extensions of older ones. In Boston, the "Big Dig" of Central Avenue was expected to require more than $15 billion to accommodate all the transit and highway facilities. In the New York metropolitan region, the Regional Plan Association advanced plans that would require an expenditure of at least $20 billion in mass transit systems alone. In Philadelphia, three major proposals for heavy rail would require a budget exceeding $7 billion. During this period there were vastly expanded budget revisions of the 1991 Interstate Surface Transportation Efficiency Act ($156 billion) and the 1998 Transportation Equity Act ($216 billion), but these federal funds were clearly not enough to accommodate the need for new mass transit systems projected throughout the country.

Public or Private?

Infrastructure needs in the early twenty-first century were based on three major considerations. The first was the nationwide anti-sprawl campaign calling for substantive improvements in mass transit and limitation of other infrastructure systems in suburban areas so that development could be significantly curbed. The second was the aging of many infrastructure systems of most older cities (such as sewerage systems), which were built in the late nineteenth and early twentieth centuries with minimal dimensions and impermanent design and materials. The third factor was the rapid growth of American urban areas and the constantly evolving technology of almost all urban infrastructure systems, including telecommunications (fiber optics), steam distribution systems (heat-resistant pipes), sewerage systems (chemical-resistant reinforced concrete), and transportation systems (automated people movers).

Primary to the construction of modern public works are the issues of who makes the decision to build it . . . and who should actually build and/or run it.

Specialists in the field considered the need of improvements and renovations in the infrastructure system of the country as the greatest challenge for the United States in the early 2000s. Many systems were simply too old to continue without major renovations (water systems, sewage networks) while others were functionally obsolete in terms of size or operations (schools, hospitals, solid waste disposal projects). The complex juxtaposition of old city centers, decaying early suburbs, expanding new suburbs, and a narrowing envelope of environmental constraints in and around the metro areas of the United States (as of many other countries of the world) produced major policy dilemmas.

Primary to the construction of modern public works are the issues of who makes the decision to build it (known as provision of services) and who should actually build and/or run it (production of services). Specialists in urban infrastructure draw a sharp distinction between provision and production of services. Although there is almost unanimous agreement that in most cases it is the government that should decide whether an infrastructure system should be provided in a city, agreement is far from certain in deciding exactly how much an infrastructure service or system should be produced through, for example, a publicly owned enterprise or a privately owned business under proper licensing as a utility or as a totally free market provision.

The production of any service or commodity is an industrial process with additional requirements of continuous technological improvements and undiminished managerial attention and skills. Additional requirements of quality, modernity, and minimization of production and distribution costs enter the discussion and impose solutions, which sometimes suggest public-sector production and distribution and sometimes private-sector involvement.

The aversion of taxpayers toward financing speculative ventures decided by civil servants at little personal risk and with dubious competence in what they decide usually holds government agencies back from improved technologies, untested managerial scenarios, and newly established social needs. This is where the private sector's entry usually is welcomed and where it is usually proven to be very useful in expanding the frontier of urban infrastructure networks. Examples of such infrastructure abound in telecommunications, health, energy, and education. In all these cases the government role stays very vigorous in regulation, in standardization, in nondiscriminatory provision, and in safety matters, but stays back from actual production.

Legislation introduced in the 1990s included extensive provisions for private sector participation in many aspects of infrastructure systems development. Under the principal of "private money for public purposes" the various programs attempt to explore the possibility of attracting private entrepreneurs to invest in projects of clear public benefit. The underlying reason in all cases is the desire to conserve public capital investment funds and to achieve additional efficiency and innovation in both the construction and operation of the new infrastructure systems components.

Another debated issue in the provision of services is the role of the three levels of government and their institutions. In theory the notion of federalism [that is, separation of duties and powers between federal and local governments] finds its perfect application in the process of building infrastructure networks in urban areas. In this scenario, the federal government establishes a national policy for the improvement and enrichment of the specific infrastructure systems and services. As part of these policies, it sponsors a national investment program in which the federal government establishes the goals, the process, the standards, and the states' and localities' roles and financial participation. The funds for many types of infrastructure projects are distributed by a formula for each state or region or on a project-by-project basis. In addition, both the 1993 Interstate Surface Transportation Efficiency Act and the Transportation Equity Act included provisions for the states and regions to exercise discretion and choice on some proportion of the funds on the basis of their local priorities and preferences. In all cases the proportion of local contribution (by state, by region, or by specific locality) is determined by the federal legislation, and it is a precondition for any further action.

Environmental Impacts

The matter of protecting the physical environment during construction and operation of infrastructure systems is an increasingly challenging issue. Most of the major environmental battles of the past have revolved around highway projects, major sewage systems, solid waste disposal sites, and water containment projects, with the conflict extending to include school sites, hospital expansion, and even mass transit lines and stations.

Environmental concerns focus on all three parts of the environment—air, land, and water—and involve concerns for human health and species retention as well as aspects of aesthetics, culture, and history. Conflicts arise over the use of nonrenewable energy resources for infrastructure operations and the sustainability of a given metropolitan region. In many cases, the arguments reach a pitch that prevents reasonable discussion and an unbiased search for solutions.

Even after all available solutions for minimizing the environmental impact of a given project have been explored, however, circumstances may require that either a major intervention on the environment will have to take place or the project must be canceled. Such has been the case on a number of solid waste disposal projects, water conservation projects, and highway projects, such as the West Side Expressway project on Manhattan Island. Nevertheless, in many other locations pressure from community and environmental groups has produced admirable solutions and very agreeable completion of infrastructure projects. Such an example is the Vine Street Expressway in Philadelphia, which was constructed as a depressed expressway with green parapets on both sides, with reasonable construction costs and very important neighborhood-friendly impacts. Still, environmental issues will continue to loom large in the future, underscoring the need for development of new and appropriate public policy guidelines and design options.

2

The US Infrastructure
Is Crumbling

Sarah Williams Goldhagen

Sarah Williams Goldhagen is the architecture critic for The New
Republic *and author of* Anxious Modernisms: Experimenta-
tion in Postwar Architectural Culture.

*America's infrastructure is badly decaying. A massive expendi-
ture is needed to provide vital maintenance to roads, bridges,
and sewage systems. Even more money is needed to meet new
infrastructure needs associated with changing population distribution. America is far behind the rest of the world, including
Canada, in its infrastructure construction. This is in large part
because America's democracy makes it hard to generate public
support for infrastructure. The federal government's decision to
leave infrastructure projects to local governments has also resulted in infrastructure neglect. The federal government needs to
step forward to take control of and oversee the improvements
that are needed.*

A quick survey of the infrastructural elements of the United
States' metropolitan regions suggests that a few might be
said to be doing tolerably well. The rest, which means those in
most of the country, are in horrendous shape. Large swaths of
our infrastructure . . . have aged to the point of gross deterio-
ration. To sense the magnitude of the problem, one need look
no further than the sobering "Infrastructure Report Card" on

the United States, which is published every few years by the country's leading professional organization in the field, the American Society of Civil Engineers [ASCE]. On the ASCE's most recent Report Card, from 2005, not a single one of fifteen categories received a grade higher than a C. Ten of the fifteen categories—including drinking water, waste-water management, navigable waterways, transit, and schools—received scores in the D range.

National Indifference

These grades are not subjective evaluations. Twenty-four of the nation's leading civil engineers analyzed hundreds of reports and studies and surveyed more than two thousand of their colleagues before assigning them. The grades are abundantly substantiated with statistics, the results of research studies, and estimates of the dollar figures necessary for remediation. The ASCE's report on the conditions in most American metropolitan regions reveals a shocking national indifference to the maintenance, upgrading, and creative reconceptualization of our own infrastructure. The ASCE Report Cards from 2003, 2001, and 1998 do not look better.

The ASCE estimates that the country would need to spend $1.6 trillion in the next five years to bring the country's infrastructure to an acceptable minimum standard.

But never mind grades. Consider facts and numbers. . . . More than 160,000 of the nation's nearly 600,000 bridges are structurally deficient or functionally obsolete, with I-35W having been one of them [the bridge in Minneapolis, Minn., that collapsed in August 2007]. The National Priorities list currently includes 1,237 toxic waste sites, and the Environmental Protection Agency has identified more than 350,000 contaminated sites that need to be cleaned up within the next three decades. Americans spend 3.5 billion hours annually stuck in traffic. In 2000, the National Education Association reported that more than $268 billion was needed to bring the nation's school facilities into good overall condition.

A quick survey of some of the ASCE's monetary estimates betrays this appalling indifference and the catastrophe that it portends. America faces an annual shortfall of $11 billion to replace aging facilities in order to comply with safe drinking water regulations, and yet as of 2005, federal funding for drinking water remained at less than 10 percent of this total. The National Park Service estimates (and probably under-estimates) a maintenance backlog of $6.1 billion. In January [2007] dozens of beaches in California were closed when heavy rains caused overflow that dumped millions of gallons of raw sewage into the waters. The number of unsafe dams rose by 33 percent between 1998 and 2005. The number of non-federally-owned dams identified as unsafe is increasing at a faster rate than those being repaired. For all the non-federally-owned dams that pose a direct risk to human life if they should fail, the ASCE estimates that $10.1 billion is needed over the next twelve years to make them safe. In sum, the ASCE estimates that the country would need to spend $1.6 trillion in the next five years to bring the country's infrastructure to an acceptable minimum standard.

New Challenges

And that's just getting what we already have back into shape. What about meeting the myriad needs of the reconfiguring world of the twenty-first century? The United States has a rapidly growing population, with certain regions, especially in the Sun Belt, requiring vast new infrastructure. Everywhere there continue to be shifts in population farther and farther from the core cities, making metropolitan regions all that much more far-flung and posing new infrastructural problems and demands. At the same time, we must cope with the phenomenon of "Shrinking Cities," the title of an exhibition at the KW Institute for Contemporary Art in Berlin in 2004 and of the indispensable three-volume catalogue that accompanied it. When a city's population significantly declines—which has happened in cities as different as New Orleans, the District of Columbia, Cleveland, Pittsburgh, and St. Louis, each of which has lost 30 to 50 percent of its inhabitants in the past half-century—large abandoned swaths of land are left behind. Do we leave de-populated cities to fend for themselves, with their boarded-up buildings deteriorating and HAZARD signs posted on building fronts, creating self-fulfilling prophecies of cities' deaths foretold? Do we neglect the opportunity to develop creative new uses for our nation's waterfronts, many of which are no longer adequate to serve as railway transit or shipping ports, and which currently sit as wastelands in sites as prominent as the west side of Manhattan? Do we ignore the thousands of brownfields—which the Environmental Protection Agency defines as "real property, the expansion, redevelopment, or reuse of which may be complicated by the presence or potential presence of a hazardous substance, pollutant, or contaminant"—that defile our purple mountains' majesty? Do we just keep building highways and airports, and more highways and airports, when in truth we must begin to reconfigure America's physical landscape to better accommodate its citizens' changing demographic profile, social habits, and economic needs?

How did the United States devolve into this perilous condition? Why has the world's greatest economic and military power neglected what is arguably its most important asset after its people (also much neglected): the infrastructure that literally constitutes its cities and metropolitan regions? How are people choosing, or being shut out of choosing, the physical configuration of their metropolitan regions, from domicile to parkland to sewage-treatment plant? The answers to these questions must come from politicians at the local, the state, and especially the federal levels; and from city planners and civil engineers; and from urban designers, architects, and landscape architects. Unless the problem is viewed with a wide-angle lens that reveals its many mutually reinforcing dimensions, it cannot be properly analyzed.

Falling Behind the World

Visit metropolitan regions in many of the rapidly developing countries in Asia, and the gross inferiority of America's physical infrastructure is immediately apparent. Highways and roads in those countries are not pitted moonscapes. Public transportation, from trains to trolleys to buses, is plentiful, in good repair, and punctual. Public structures of all kinds—from governmental and civic buildings to public parks and urban plazas to "streetscape" elements such as pedestrian bridges and roadway lighting fixtures—are of immensely higher design quality and in immensely better shape. At every turn, a citizen moving through the built environment of these countries sees and uses physically embodied signs communicating to them that in their society, public life matters.

> *The nature of the American democratic system discourages the long-term planning, the commitment to public investment, and the vertical coordination of federal, state, and local initiatives that most advanced industrial countries enjoy.*

But forget, if you wish, the vast infrastructural building taking place across economically exploding Asia and the Middle East. Look no farther than Europe or Canada, areas in what used to be called the industrialized world, where metropolitan regions are facing the same problems of demographic shifts, higher labor costs, and aging infrastructure that we face in the United States. Again and again we find examples of metropolitan regions that have successfully risen to these challenges. Two of the most extraordinary recent success stories are Barcelona and Vancouver. Barcelona, in preparation for the Summer Olympics in 1992, remade itself by hiring world-class city planners, urban designers, architects, and civil engineers to rehabilitate its aged urban center, construct an Olympic Village that has become a new settlement in its metropolitan region, construct a new ring road, and reclaim its waterfront by transforming miles upon miles of beaches into parkland with bicycle paths, marinas, swimming areas, urban plazas, and high-quality residential fabric—all accessible by public transportation. And Vancouver's physical remaking in the past two decades has been so remarkable that it has become a phenomenon, a brand: the "Vancouver Miracle," a city that, twenty years ago, was an emptied-out downtown littered with disused industrial lots and is today a lively, high-density, twenty-four-hour city filled with attractively designed high-rise residential and office towers, well-preserved historic buildings, plentiful public parks, and vibrant cultural institutions. Vancouver is currently the fastest-growing residential downtown in North America.

Infrastructure is an amorphous topic. Building it and maintaining it is staggeringly expensive. In the eyes of many voters, elected officials, and professional stewards of the built environment, maintaining it, trying to visualize what it should be or could be, is just plain boring. Re-orienting ourselves toward our infrastructure and bringing it up to date requires clearing away multiple political, social, and conceptual obstacles. As this past spring's exhibitions on Robert Moses [a leader of City Planning in New York] in New York City made clear about the politics of American infrastructure, the nature of the American democratic system discourages the long-term planning, the commitment to public investment, and the vertical coordination of federal, state, and local initiatives that most advanced industrial countries enjoy, which are fundamental to the establishment, maintenance, and upgrading of the existing infrastructure, not to mention the initiation of new projects.

Not Willing to Pay

American citizens know that they and their children need safe bridges, clean drinking water, public school buildings that do not force classes to convene in hallways or leak or cause sick building syndrome, and clean and healthy parks so that playing children are not forced onto city streets or toxic waste sites. Yet voters are exquisitely prone to sticker shock, and large-scale infrastructural projects—a new mass-transit line, a new park or waterway system, a bridge—cost an extraordinary amount of money. Indeed, the projected dollar amounts themselves are often enough to cause the political equivalent of what psychologists of trauma call dissociation. (Did you say $14.6 *billion* for Boston's Central Artery project?) Even smaller-scale projects—a new public school, a waterfront park (such as Pittsburgh's $22 million Allegheny Riverfront Park, or the recently completed $85 million Olympic Sculpture Park in Seattle), an urban public plaza (such as the $650 million re-tooling of Lincoln Center in New York City to make it more user-friendly and accessible to the public)—seem fantastically expensive to anyone who has no experience of planning and managing costs for any major construction project—in other words, to nearly everyone, including nearly every one of our voting citizens.

When a proposed tax or budget item can be specifically linked to the officials whom voters elect to their own state or local offices, the political disincentives to address a metropolitan region's infrastructural needs are enormous. Funding maintenance for existing infrastructure is doubly challenging because there is not even the political reward of a shining new public amenity. If Madame Governor proposes a good or necessary infrastructure project, should she keep trying to push the project through when the bidding process is complete and her constituents balk at its projected cost? Should she do so if the ultimate cost is her job? Should she do so with the knowledge that, at any point along the way, from conception to design to construction, determined and vocal detractors can point to the mounting dollar signs, and portray that project as a sinkhole for taxpayer money, and derail it?

Even in the heyday of American infrastructure-building, from 1930 to 1970, it took an imperious wheeler-dealer such as Robert Moses to take maximal advantage of the funds that the federal government was making available to American cities: owing to Moses, for example, New York City received more than twice the Title I funds for slum clearance of any other city in the country. Robert Caro, Moses's biographer, who was simultaneously fascinated and revolted by Moses's labyrinthine anti-democratic conception of his calling, conceded in *The Power Broker* that "the problem of constructing large-scale public works in a crowded urban setting, where such works impinge upon the lives of or displace thousands of voters, is one that democracy has not yet solved." American democracy, that is.

Worsening Neglect

The neglect of infrastructure has dramatically worsened since the 1970s, for two reasons. First, the country has undergone a structural transformation from city-suburb-exurb-farmland, a constellation that does not necessarily conflict with the tripartite local-state-federal structure of our government, into metropolitan regions, a constellation that does conflict with that structure. We are stuck with the existing political, legal, and institutional structures of states (usually bigger than metropolitan areas) and municipalities (smaller and self-interested) through which almost everything must be organized and funneled. Neither is the right kind of entity for managing a metropolitan region, but together they inevitably organize our thinking and, more important, our policy planning, which turns out to be too unfocused (in the case of states) or too hyper-focused (in the case of municipalities).

Owing to the disincentives to address the country's infrastructure that are built into the American democratic system . . . the political obstacles to taking America's infrastructural problems seriously are enormous.

Second, the federal government has increasingly fobbed off the responsibility for maintaining and upgrading the country's infrastructure onto state and local governments, which bear the legal obligation to attend to their regions' infrastructure but are systemically constituted in such a manner that only rarely can they command the financial resources adequate to accomplish the necessary tasks. A Congressional Budget Office [CBO] study reveals that an immediate and steady decline in federal spending on infrastructure as a percentage of GDP [gross domestic product, a measure of the economy's total production] began with [Ronald] Reagan's first budget and continues straight downhill, with the average annual amount in 1982–1998 being 29 percent less than in 1965–1981. While in the earlier period the average was .93 percent of GDP, in the last year of the CBO's study the downward trend had brought spending all the way down to .57 percent of GDP—a drop of almost 40 percent. Federal spending on infrastructure as a percentage of all federal spending between these two periods, which include Republican and Democratic administrations, declined even more, by 33 percent. And states and municipalities have not picked up the slack: state and local spending throughout these years has hovered around a little less than 2 percent of GDP. Max Sawicky of the Economic Policy Institute uses somewhat different measurements, though his figures for public net investment in physical capital come up to 2006: he estimates that for the ten years between 1959 and 1969, public net investment in physical capital was about 2.6 percent of GDP; but for the last ten years it has been about 1.1 percent.

Without a large federal role, infrastructural needs cannot be effectively addressed, in part because the American political system has always made it difficult for state and local governments to do so, and in part because metropolitan regions cut across municipal and sometimes even state lines. This is one of those tasks that only the federal government can accomplish. A dramatic example of why state and local governments cannot go it alone on infrastructure building comes from New Mexico, which has recently completed a new four-lane highway: when that new highway reaches the Colorado state border, it dies into two lanes, because the state of Colorado has not coughed up the funds to continue it. Owing to the disincentives to address the country's infrastructure that are built into the American democratic system—and to the rightward shove of our governance in the last twenty years, which has militated against even discussing, let alone addressing, large-scale public needs—the political obstacles to taking America's infrastructural problems seriously are enormous. Shouldn't we think about our country's physical plant in terms not that different from our legal and regulatory systems in general—as a necessary foundation for the social and economic health and growth of this country; requiring substantial federal leadership and funding? We need a national infrastructure for infrastructure.

3

The US Infrastructure Is Not Crumbling

Charles Lane

Charles Lane is a staff writer for the Washington Post.

Conventional wisdom holds that the US infrastructure is in a state of catastrophic disrepair. However, the truth is that in comparison to other countries of similar size, the US does an excellent job of maintaining its roads, bridges, and airports. While the US could probably stand to spend more money on infrastructure, large infrastructure expenditures are often counterproductive and plagued by corruption. Infrastructure spending needs to be undertaken with care. Claims that there is an infrastructure crisis when there is none make for bad public policy.

All right-thinking people agree: America's infrastructure is in bad shape. The only debate is over how bad. Is our infrastructure "increasingly third-world"—per *Slate's* Jacob Weisberg—or a "national disgrace" and "global embarrassment"—as Barry Ritholtz suggested in a recent column for *The [Washington] Post?*

Clean and Safe

Data seem to support this gloomy conventional wisdom. In the World Economic Forum's (WEF) latest Global Competitiveness Report, the United States' infrastructure ranked 23rd, behind that of Malaysia and Barbados. Barbados!

The American Society of Civil Engineers gives America's system a "D," as President [Barack] Obama often notes in support of his jobs bill, which provides $50 billion for transportation infrastructure and $10 billion to capitalize a national infrastructure bank.

The challenge of building and maintaining first-rate roads, bridges, railroads, airports and seaports in a country like the United States is extraordinary—and so is the degree to which the United States succeeds.

So how come my family and I traveled thousands of miles on both the east and west coasts last summer without actually seeing any crumbling roads or airports? On the whole, the highways and byways were clean, safe and did not remind me of the Third World countries in which I have lived or worked. Should I believe the pundits or my own eyes?

For all its shortcomings, U.S. infrastructure is still among the most advanced in the world—if not the most advanced. I base this not on selective personal experience but on the same data alarmists cite.

Meeting the Challenge

The contiguous United States (that is, excluding Alaska and Hawaii) cover 3.1 million square miles, including deserts, mountain ranges, rivers and two oceanic coastlines. In a world of vast dictatorships (China), tiny democracies (Switzerland) and everything in between, from Malta to Mexico, the challenge of building and maintaining first-rate roads, bridges, railroads, airports and seaports in a country like the United States is extraordinary—and so is the degree to which the United States succeeds.

When you compare America's WEF rankings with those of the 19 other largest countries, it stands second only to Canada, which is lightly populated—and whose infrastructure is linked with ours.

Among the 20 most populous countries, the United States ranks behind France, Germany and Japan, in that order. This would seem to confirm the case for U.S. inferiority in the developed world.

But France and Germany, in addition to being substantially smaller than the United States, are part of the European Union [E.U.], a borderless single market from the Baltic Sea to the Black Sea. Sure enough, when you average out the scores of all 27 E.U. nations, the United States beats them by a clear margin.

The WEF produced its rankings based on a survey in which business executives were asked to rate their respective countries' infrastructure on an ascending scale of 1 to 7.

Barbados's 5.8 average score means that paradise's execs are a smidgen happier with their infrastructure than are their American counterparts, who gave the United States an average score of 5.7. This is a "national disgrace"? Barbados has one commercial airport. The United States has more than 500.

Though roads, rails and levees represent huge, upfront capital expenditures, the long-term benefits are often difficult to calculate objectively.

The WEF asked executives to rate "railroad infrastructure," without distinguishing between freight (which excels in the United States) and passenger (which does not).

Perhaps the survey's subjectivity accounts for odd results such as Guatemala outranking Italy. Or that the U.S. score plunged below 6.0 for the first time in 2008—proof of a sudden drop in the actual quality of our roads and bridges, or merely an indicator of the general despondency that hit U.S. businesses along with the Great Recession?

And while that D from the American Society of Civil Engineers is undoubtedly sincere, the organization has a vested interest in greater infrastructure spending, which means more work for engineers. The engineers' lobby has given America's infrastructure a D in every one of its report cards going back to 1998, except for 2001, when the mark was D-plus.

Top-notch though it is, the U.S. infrastructure could use an upgrade; by their very nature, roads, bridges and the rest require constant maintenance. The effort could boost both current employment and the economy's capacity to grow in the future.

But it's not just a matter of turning on the money tap and letting it flow. Though roads, rails and levees represent huge, upfront capital expenditures, the long-term benefits are often difficult to calculate objectively. The whole business is fraught with uncertainty, trade-offs and pork-barrel politics.

Nor are the economics of public works simple. After its economic bubble burst, Japan tried to restart growth with more than $6 trillion in infrastructure spending between 1991 and 2008. It ended up with little to show for it but a swollen national debt and lots of bridges to nowhere.

The United States probably needs more infrastructure spending. It also needs a serious debate about how much cash to invest and how to invest it. Alarmism promotes the former, not the latter.

4

Federal Infrastructure Investment Is Needed to Fuel an Economic Recovery

Robert Kuttner

Robert Kuttner is the co-founder and co-editor of The American Prospect, *the co-founder of the Economic Policy Institute, and a columnist for* The Boston Globe.

The US economy continues to be mired in unemployment. In order to push up job growth, the government should start a massive public works program funded by taxes on the wealthy and on financial transactions. It is true that there is already a large deficit, but trying to cut deficits in a recession will merely cause further contraction. Unfortunately, Republicans oppose public works spending, and Democrats and President Barack Obama have also been reluctant to push forward the necessary programs. As a result, any recovery is likely to be hobbled.

The dismal May [2011] employment numbers show the U.S. economy is sputtering, and those who were hoping for a summer of economic green shoots have been kidding themselves.

Public Investment Is Needed

From February to April, private employers added an average of almost 220,000 jobs—that's progress, though only at about half the pace the economy needs to get back to pre-recession employment levels. But in May, the number fell to just 83,000 new private-sector jobs, and that number drops to 54,000 if you net out the jobs lost to continued layoffs at all levels of government. Manufacturing employment had also ticked up slightly, but in May the industry resumed its long-term trend of shedding jobs. Economists had hoped that increased consumer spending signaled a stronger economy, but it mainly reflected higher prices for fuel and food.

Lately, the media and the Washington hothouse have been busy debating deficit reduction. Those are the wrong debates. Deficit reduction does nothing for job growth, and is economically perverse at this stage of a weak recovery. Continued high unemployment will wreck President Barack Obama's re-election chances; even more important, it will condemn the economic prospects of an entire generation. It's not as if we are doomed to this future. There are solutions, but they are off the radar screen of mainstream politics.

What the economy needs to fully recover is a massive . . . infrastructure and jobs program.

For starters, we need a large-scale program of public investment to improve our infrastructure. The American Society of Civil Engineers puts the basic price tag for deferred maintenance at $2.2 trillion. That refers to collapsing water and sewer systems, roads, bridges, public buildings—it doesn't even include 21st century infrastructure like smart-grid power systems . . . , universal broadband and green energy.

But beside providing for basic maintenance needs, what the economy needs to fully recover is a massive—and I mean massive—infrastructure and jobs program financed by surtaxes on wealthy individuals and on windfall financial-sector profits, including taxes on profits from short-term financial trades. We could also get upwards of $200 billion a year from tax enforcement, mainly on trans-national evasion used by

America's wealthiest. Some of the funds for this program could also come from winding down the gratuitous wars [in Iraq and Afghanistan] we're currently engaged in. And some could even come from a modest increase in short-term deficits.

The order of magnitude of the public investment program should be at least half a trillion dollars a year, for at least five years, and more if that doesn't solve the problem. We would not hesitate to spend this kind of money and levy surtaxes if America found itself in a serious war. It was the economic side-effects of the massive WWII program of tax, borrow, and invest that finally pulled America out of the Great Depression—and powered the postwar boom.

But even though we face a national emergency, it seems impossible to summon up the political resolve for this kind of collective enterprise absent the total mobilization of a major war.

Economic history shows that when the private sector is too traumatized to revive economic activity and employment, public investment is the only way to jump start a full recovery.

The jobs problem might seem intractable because we already have a deficit of around 10 percent of GDP [Gross Domestic Product, a measure of the economy's total production] and the Fed [Federal Reserve Board] has already pushed down short-term interest rates to close to zero. According to the conventional view, policymakers are out of tricks. Even worse, the policy elite is focused on the idea that deficit reduction will somehow produce more jobs.

Deficit Reduction Does Not Create Jobs

We have some Republican politicians like Paul Ryan calling for huge spending cuts in the name of deficit reduction—

almost all of which would go for tax cuts, leaving the deficit largely unchanged. We have other Republican politicians like Tim Pawlenty calling for actual budget balance, which would drive the economy even further into a hole.

And on the Democratic side, we have inconsistent policy and messaging. In his important April 13 [2011] speech at George Washington University, President Obama devoted part of his remarks to brave words about the importance of fairness and social investment—but the other half was the conventional plea for fiscal responsibility. Obama's budget proposal, at least, is a lot less draconian than that of the Republicans, but it will not be enough either to fix the economy.

This apparent policy paralysis is mainly a reflection of how much damage was done by the financial collapse.

What we face is not an ordinary macro-economic challenge of recovering from an ordinary recession. There is huge structural damage—everything from the loss of trillions of dollars of household net worth due to the housing collapse to weakened bank balance sheets to an epidemic of outsourcing as corporations try to cut their own costs. It all adds up to a massive deflationary drag. The proof is that neither zero interest rates nor double digit deficits—which ordinarily would provide very rapid growth—are curing the problem. But the government still has the remedy of large-scale, job-intensive public investment. Economic history shows that when the private sector is too traumatized to revive economic activity and employment, public investment is the only way to jump start a full recovery.

Obviously, the Republicans will never to agree to a program of large public investment. But Obama ought to propose one. It would be far better, both for Obama and for the country, to have the 2012 election as a referendum on jobs rather than an arcane and counterproductive debate about two brands of budget cutting.

5

Federal Infrastructure Spending Will Not Fuel an Economic Recovery

Veronique de Rugy

Veronique de Rugy is a senior research fellow at the Mercatus Center at Georgetown University and a monthly columnist for Reason, *a magazine that covers politics, culture, and ideas.*

Infrastructure spending is not a good way to stimulate the economy. Economists do not agree that infrastructure spending creates a powerful impetus to growth. In addition, infrastructure spending is slow to enter the economy, is not targeted towards areas hardest hit by the recession, and creates high costs long after stimulus is needed. This is especially the case because infrastructure projects are often plagued by cost overruns and corruption. Moreover, it is not the government's job to spend on infrastructure problems, which are better handled by local governments or by privatization.

As we know, one of the things the president [Barack Obama] will call for tonight [September 2011] is more infrastructure spending. We have heard many times that infrastructure spending, in one form or another, is the key to growth and job creation—and, in the president's defense, he certainly isn't the only one who refers to stimulus and government spending as "investing" in infrastructure.

Doubtful Benefits

No one disputes that American public works need improving, and economists have long recognized the value of infrastructure. Roads, bridges, airports, and canals are the conduits through which goods are exchanged. However, whatever its merits, infrastructure spending is unlikely to provide much of a stimulus—and it certainly won't provide the boost that the president will promise the American people tonight.

> *For spending to be stimulative, it has to be timely, targeted, and temporary. Infrastructure spending isn't any of that.*

For one thing, even though Mark Zandi [a leading economist] claims that the bang for the buck is significant when the government spends $1 on infrastructure ($1.44 in growth), that's just his opinion. The reality is that economists are far from having reached a consensus on what the actual return on infrastructure spending is. As economists Eric Leeper, Todd Walker, and Shu-Chum Yang put it in a recent paper for the IMF [International Monetary Fund]: "Economists have offered an embarrassingly wide range of estimated multipliers." Among respected economists, some find larger multipliers and some find negative ones. . . .

Second, according to Keynesian economists,[1] for spending to be stimulative, it has to be timely, targeted, and temporary. Infrastructure spending isn't any of that. That's because infrastructure projects involve planning, bidding, contracting, construction, and evaluation. Only $28 billion of the $45 billion in DOT [US Department of Transportation] money included in the stimulus has been spent so far.

---

1. John Maynard Keynes was an economist who argued that government spending could spur economic growth.

We know that the stimulus money wasn't targeted toward the areas that were hit the most by the recession, but even if the funding *were* targeted, it still might not be stimulative. First, the same level of job poaching [that is, people who already have jobs move to take the new jobs created by the stimulus] from existing jobs would have happened; construction workers tend to be highly specialized, and skilled workers rarely suffer from high unemployment. Many of the areas that were hardest hit by the recession are in decline because they have been producing goods and services that are not, and will never be, in great demand. The overall value added by improving their roads is probably a lot less than that of new infrastructure in growing areas that might have relatively little unemployment but do have great demand for more roads, schools, and other types of long-term infrastructure.

Long-Term Costs

As for being temporary—which stimulus spending needs to be to work—what the president will propose tonight is likely to cost the American people money for a very long time.

It's a mistake to assume that it is the role of the federal government to pay for roads and highway expansions.

Infrastructure spending tends to suffer from massive cost overruns, waste, fraud, and abuse. A comprehensive study examining 20 nations on five continents ("Underestimating Costs in Public Works Projects: Error or Lie?" by Bent Flyvbjerg, Mette K. Skamris Holm, and Søren L. Buhl) found that nine out of ten public-works projects come in over budget. Cost overruns routinely range from 50 to 100 percent of the original estimate. For rail, the average cost is 44.7 percent greater than the estimated cost at the time the decision was made. For bridges and tunnels, the equivalent figure is 33.8 percent, for roads 20.4 percent.

I should also add that I think it's a mistake to assume that it is the role of the federal government to pay for roads and highway expansions. With very few exceptions, most roads, bridges, and even highways are local projects (state projects at most) by nature. The federal government shouldn't have anything to do with them.

In fact, I would argue that taxpayers and consumers would be better off if these activities were privatized. And if states aren't ready for privatization, they can do what Indiana did a few years back when it leased its main highways to a private company for $4 billion. The state was $4 billion richer, and it was still the owner of the highway. Consumers in Indiana were better off, because the deal saved money. Experiences in other countries have also shown that privatization leads to innovation and reduced congestion. . . .

Spending more on infrastructure right now, and expecting miracles from it, is a very risky bet.

6

Investment in Infrastructure Makes Fiscal Sense in a Recession

Ezra Klein

Ezra Klein is a columnist for the Washington Post *and* Bloomberg, *and a contributor to MSNBC.*

America's infrastructure is badly in need of repair. Fortunately, the recession has lowered the cost of building materials, so investing in construction now is a bargain. In addition, the construction industry was badly hit by the recession, so spending on construction is strongly stimulative. Also, interest rates are low, which means that the cost of borrowing for construction is very cheap. It is true that infrastructure spending will increase the deficit, but putting off needed repairs is just another way of going into debt. Finally, spending on infrastructure now will increase economic growth. Thus, the recession is the right time to spend on infrastructure improvement.

People say the government should be run more like a business. So imagine yourself as CEO [chief executive officer]. Your bridges are crumbling. Your air-traffic control system doesn't use GPS [global positioning system]. The [American] Society of Civil Engineers [a professional organization of engineers who focus on design, construction, and maintenance of infrastructure] gave your infrastructure a D and estimated that you need to make more than $2 trillion in repairs and upgrades. Sorry, chief. No one said being CEO was easy.

Too Modest

But there's good news, too. Because of the recession [of 2007–2009], construction materials are cheap. So is labor. And your borrowing costs? They've never been lower. That means a dollar of investment today will go much further than it would have five years ago—or than it's likely to go five years from now. So what do you do? If you're thinking like a CEO, the answer is easy: you invest.

That's what the [Barack Obama] administration is proposing to do. But their plan is too modest. The $50 billion bump in infrastructure spending it outlined is only for surface transportation. And as for our water systems, schools, and levees? This is not a time for half measures. It's a rare opportunity to do what we need to do—and save money doing it.

There has never been a better moment for America to rebuild.

In 2009, Congress passed the American Recovery and Reinvestment Act—the stimulus. Billions went to the Transportation Department to improve our roads, rails, and runways. That money was, in turn, given to the states, which drew up lists of what they needed to do and how much it would cost.

When the Feds checked in on the funds, what they found shocked them. The projects were coming in at about 20 percent less than estimated. The Transportation Department looked at the share that went to the Federal Aviation Administration [FAA] for runway repairs. The money the FAA thought would complete 300 projects was going to finish 367. The stimulus, the Feds realized, had blundered into an incredible deal: the recession was driven by the collapse of the construction sector. People who built things were now out of work. The materials used for building things were now on fire sale.

The companies that organized the building of things were suddenly desperate for jobs. As a result, building things was suddenly dirt cheap.

And it still is. Unemployment in the construction sector is at 17 percent—and that doesn't even count the construction workers who've given up looking for jobs. "There's work that needs to be done," Larry Summers, outgoing chairman of the National Economic Council, told me. "There are people there to do it. It seems a crime for the two not to be brought together."

Now Is the Time to Borrow

As for debt, delaying a dollar of needed repairs is no different from racking up a dollar the government owes. "You run a deficit both when you borrow money and when you defer maintenance," Summers says. "Either way, you're imposing a cost on future generations." Plus, if America has to borrow money, now is the time. The interest rate on 10-year Treasuries is less than 3 percent—the lowest it has been *since the 1950s.* So a dollar of debt is cheap, and a dollar of infrastructure investment goes far.

We'll have to pay down that debt, of course. But part of paying down the debt is increasing economic growth. What worries the market is the size of our debt against the size of our GDP [gross domestic product, a measure of the size of the economy]. If our economy grows faster than our debt, then our debt, in the eyes of the market, gets smaller. But if our economy is going to grow that fast, we'll need an infrastructure able to support that kind of growth. Tomorrow's energy contracts won't be won by the country with yesterday's energy grid.

The problem is that the process by which we choose infrastructure projects is embarrassing. About 10 percent of infrastructure spending comes from earmarks. Most of the rest depends on a formula in which the government just hands money to the states. There's no requirement for cost-benefit analysis. The decisions are horribly politicized. If taxpayers are making a huge investment in our nation's infrastructure, then we're owed an assurance that policymakers are choosing the best projects. That suggests a grand compromise in which more infrastructure money is tied to reforms ensuring a better process for spending that money.

There has never been a better moment for America to re-build. An unlikely and unwelcome array of forces has con-verged to match our needs and the economy's bargains almost perfectly. The only question is if we'll run our government like a business, alert to good opportunities, or if we'll run it as we have been, squabbling among ourselves while things get worse.

How about it, chief?

7

Investment in Infrastructure Does Not Make Fiscal Sense in a Recession

Charles Scaliger

Charles Scaliger is a teacher and freelance writer whose work often appears in The New American.

President Barack Obama's infrastructure spending program has done little to improve the economy. The nation should think twice before embarking on another round of infrastructure spending. The government loves large-scale infrastructure projects, but usually they do not confer the promised benefits and cost huge amounts of money. In the current fiscal situation, with high deficits and a weakened economy, the United States should not be spending vast sums on ill-conceived infrastructure projects which the public cannot afford.

If it is true, as Albert Einstein is alleged to have said, that insanity consists of doing the same thing over and over again and expecting different results, then President [Barack] Obama and his advisors may well be channeling the great 20th Century physicist. After all, the President is neither chastened nor enlightened following the monumental failure of his multitrillion dollar efforts to stimulate the economy by spending taxpayer money. As his September 6 [2010] speech at the Milwaukee, Wisconsin, Laborfest attested, he's going to try it yet again.

Charles Scaliger, "Obama's New Stimulus Target: Infrastructure," *New American* online, September 6, 2010. TheNewAmerican.com. Copyright © 2010 by The New American.

Infrastructure and Redistribution

In a widely anticipated pre-election initiative, Obama announced a new $50 billion dollar program to rebuild America's allegedly ailing transportation infrastructure, apparently in the fond delusion that American voters are preparing to vent their electoral wrath on Washington for not spending enough of their hard-earned dollars.

We are still left to wonder whether, in this era of buckling finances, we ought to authorize still more expensive public works projects.

"Over the next six years," the President told an enthusiastic union crowd, many of whom would doubtless benefit directly from the welter of new proposed construction projects, "we are going to rebuild 150,000 miles of our roads—enough to circle the world six times. We're going to lay and maintain 4,000 miles of our railways—enough to stretch coast-to-coast. We're going to restore 150 miles of runways and advance a next generation air-traffic control system to reduce travel time and delays for American travelers."

The proposal would include the installation of a new high-speed rail system linking Milwaukee with Madison, the state capital, part of an ambitious program to create a national high-speed rail system that would allegedly save time, money, and air quality. And to administer the funds for this latest stimulus boondoggle, a new permanent "infrastructure bank" would be set up "to leverage federal dollars and focus on the smartest investments," whatever that might mean.

Investing in infrastructure has always been a favorite conceit of the redistributionally-minded, from hardcore Marxists to modern American Presidents with their varying flavors of socialism Lite. This is partly because transportation, involving as it does matters of interstate commerce and eminent domain, is one of the few things that most people agree government should have some hand in. No one has yet found and managed to put into practice a successful system of fully privatized roads, for example (although America has managed to maintain some semblance of privatization in some sectors of mass transportation, like airlines, where many other countries have insisted on state ownership).

As for transportation spending itself, roads, airlines, and railways aren't necessarily the unalloyed fiscal benefits they're chalked up to be.

But even if the federal government has some pretense of constitutional authority for rebuilding roads, railroads, and the like (and the authority is tenuous, if we take into account that the modern expansive interpretation of the "interstate commerce" clause[1] in no way reflects the Founders' sentiments, [Alexander] Hamilton possibly excepted), we are still left to wonder whether, in this era of buckling finances, we ought to authorize still more expensive public works projects.

No Real Effect

The recent economic stimulus efforts have impacted the economy in roughly the same way that a boy tossing stones into a lake expects to raise the water level: The water is agitated with each impact, but the lake, determined to find its own level, looks the same once the ripples have died away. In like manner, the Obama stimulus monies stirred the surface of the economy for a few short months, prompting economist-myrmidons to proclaim the end of the recession and the beginning of new, albeit sluggish, growth.

---

1. Article 1, Section 8 of the Constitution, which gives Congress the power to regulate economic activity between states. It has been interpreted to give the federal government broad power over economic activity.

But now that the stimulus money has worked its way through the system, anointing the palms of government employees and contractors at the expense of everyone else, the economy looks no different. Unemployment is unchanged, savings are depleted, credit has dried up, and nobody's hiring. While the atmosphere of panic has receded, it's beginning to dawn on just about everyone who will cast a ballot this fall that, two years and several trillion dollars into the Obama presidency, things have not improved a whit and, without a fresh approach, may soon get a lot worse, given all the new debt America has to service.

As for transportation spending itself, roads, airlines, and railways aren't necessarily the unalloyed fiscal benefits they're chalked up to be. Two generations ago, the French and British governments launched a visionary new program to usher jet transportation into the supersonic age. The much-ballyhooed SST (supersonic transport, better known as the Concorde) turned transatlantic flight into a thrilling, three hour adrenalin rush—for those willing and able to spend more than $10,000.00 to fly a route that, for a few hours more and in considerably greater comfort and less noise, cost a few hundred dollars. The Concorde never came close to living up to its promise, and three decades and countless billions of dollars of taxpayer subsidies later, it was finally abandoned after a Concorde literally went down in flames at Charles de Gaul airport in July 2000.

What about high-speed rail travel? Who could possibly object to state-of-the-art trains rushing along maglev rails at speeds comparable to some passenger aircraft, conveying commuters from city center to city center without the hassles of airport traffic and security? For the record, high-speed trains are a lot of fun to ride on, as anyone who has ridden America's only high-speed rail (the Acela that plies the northeastern corridor from Washington to Boston) will attest. But they're also very expensive, both to ride and to run, leaving aside the vast expenditures to set them up. It is both cheaper and faster to fly from D.C. to Boston, even factoring in getting to and from the airport. France and Japan have both had vaunted high speed rail systems for decades, which have become centerpieces in their respective national tourism industries but have done nothing to actually enrich the French and Japanese economies.

> *What the upcoming elections will hopefully highlight ... is America's need to confront fiscal and financial realities instead of continuing on her post-boom government spending spree.*

Much the same could be said of more mundane expenditures, like highway upgrades, which routinely go overtime and over budget, and are usually driven less by genuine economic need than by political gamesmanship—Alaska's infamous "Bridge to Nowhere" is but one all-too-typical example of the way politicians love to pork up road and bridge expropriations. And lest we forget, modern freeways were invented in the 1930s by another gang of "visionary" politicians needing a high-profile distraction from global economic ills and internal political turmoil—Hitler and his Nazis.

Politicians like President Obama love grand public transportation projects—they are eye-catching, visionary, and a very high-profile way of putting people to work with government money (those "Your taxpayer dollars at work" signs, in all their varieties, were invented to garland such projects). Aside from the literal monuments they erect for themselves, there is nothing so grandiose as a public transportation initiative, whether a new freeway named after the Congressman who spent the money to build it or the latest eye-popping air or rail technology.

The Bottom Line

But the bottom line is always the bottom line. The fact that we know how to build 10-lane freeways, supersonic transports, high-speed rails, or ultramodern cable-stayed bridges to replace fuddy-duddy highways, conventional passenger jets, diesel trains, and suspension bridges does not necessarily mean that we should. The know-how exists for many things that could be done with resources, but that we cannot afford—sending people back to the moon, for example.

What the upcoming elections [of 2010] will hopefully highlight (among many other things) is America's need to confront fiscal and financial realities instead of continuing on her post-boom government spending spree intended [to] bring back the illusory glory of a boom that can never be recaptured nor repeated via government intervention.

None of which is to say that America must be content with second-tier status. It means that a country's greatness—ours or any others—has little to do with the ability of its politicians to spend money on public works. The illusion that national greatness flows from public greatness, as measured by politicians' generosity with other people's money, is a misconception at least as old as ancient Babylon. America is great first and foremost because of her national character, and her material prowess has come not as a consequence of a visionary "enlightened despot" like Peter the Great or an ambitious dynasty like the Tudors, but because of the way she has liberated her citizenry from the chains of absolutism.

But the Obamas and others who invest their faith not in freedom but in the state are unlikely ever to grasp such a notion. Nor are they likely to change their ways until they are corrected by those of us who pay the bills they run up.

8

The Minneapolis Bridge Collapse Reveals the Nation's Deferred Maintenance

Ron Scherer

Ron Scherer is a staff writer for the Christian Science Monitor.

The collapse of a highway bridge over the Mississippi River in Minneapolis highlights the need for better examination and maintenance of America's infrastructure. Other accidents in recent years, including the eruption of a steam pipe in Manhattan, show that infrastructure maintenance should be improved. Bridge maintenance is especially important, since bridges can corrode and deteriorate quickly. The American Society of Civil Engineers has criticized the country's maintenance of its infrastructure, and has advocated increased spending to preserve bridges and other infrastructure.

The tragic rush-hour collapse in Minneapolis of the I-35W Bridge over the Mississippi River is again forcing a reexamination of the nation's approach to maintaining and inspecting critical infrastructure.

Tragic Infrastructure Disasters

According to engineers, the nation is spending only about two-thirds as much as it should be to keep dams, levees, highways, and bridges safe. The situation is more urgent now because many such structures were designed 40 or 50 years ago, before Americans were driving weighty SUVs and truckers were lugging tandem loads.

It all adds up to a poor grade: The American Society of Civil Engineers [ASCE, a professional organization for infrastructure engineers] gave the nation a D in 2005, the latest report available, after assessing 12 categories of infrastructure ranging from rails and roads to wastewater treatment and dams.

America's 577,000 bridges are of particular concern because they are subject to corrosion.

"One of America's great assets is its infrastructure, but if you don't invest it deteriorates," says Patrick Natale, executive director of ASCE.

Among scores of recent examples:

- Last month, a 100-year-old steam pipe erupted in midtown Manhattan, killing one man and causing millions of dollars in lost business.

- The inadequacies of levees in New Orleans became horrifyingly clear in the aftermath of hurricane Katrina. The city is still recovering.

- In 2003, the Silver Lake Dam in Michigan failed, causing $100 million in damage.

America's 577,000 bridges are of particular concern because they are subject to corrosion. According to the website of Nondestructive Testing (NDT), which advocates not damaging structures during testing, the average lifespan of a bridge is about 70 years. Bridges are inspected visually every two years. However, NDT notes, "it is not uncommon for a fisherman, canoeist, and other passerby to alert officials to major damage that may have occurred between inspections."

Rated Deficient

In the federal government's rating system, any bridge that scores less than 80—on a scale of 1 to 100—is in need of rehabilitation. A bridge scoring below 50 should undergo reconstruction under federal guidelines. In 2004, 26.7 percent of US bridges, urban and rural, were rated deficient, down from 27.5 percent in 2002, according to the US Department of Transportation (DOT).

Minnesota's record is far better, with only 12.2 percent of its bridges falling into the deficient or obsolete categories.

Federal officials were quick to point out that those designations don't mean the bridges are unsafe.

"None of those ratings said there was any kind of danger," US Transportation Secretary Mary Peters said in Minneapolis on Thursday. The ratings are used to point out deficiencies or overhauls that need to be conducted in the future.

State officials were in the process of completing a third inspection . . . when the bridge collapsed Wednesday afternoon at the height of rush hour.

Most bridge collapses occur from an obvious cause: an earthquake or a barge running into bridge supports. On rare occasions, however, bridges have collapsed for less obvious reasons. In 1983 in Greenwich, Conn., the Mianus River Bridge collapsed, killing three people. A federal investigation blamed excessive accumulation of corrosion on a hangar pin, a key part of the bridge.

In the case of the Minneapolis bridge collapse, the National Transportation Safety Board [NTSB] will lead the investigation. Its investigators were also on the scene to begin to piece together what had caused the collapse.

"It is much too early in this investigation to know what happened," NTSB Chairman Mark Rosenker said Thursday

[August 2007]. The first step is to reassemble the pieces of the bridge like a jigsaw puzzle to figure out what triggered the collapse, he said.

State inspection officials had inspected the bridge twice since the federal government rated the bridge "structurally deficient" but concluded the bridge was safe. State officials were in the process of completing a third inspection—interrupted because of construction on the bridge—when the bridge collapsed Wednesday afternoon at the height of rush hour.

As many as 30 people were missing as of press time Thursday.

Longtime Concerns

Concerns about the bridge go back at least six years.

A 2001 report by the University of Minnesota, Department of Civil Engineering, stated, "Concern about fatigue cracking in the deck is heightened by a lack of redundancy in the main truss system. Only two planes of the main trusses support the eight lanes of traffic. The truss is determinate and the joints are theoretically pinned. Therefore, if one member were severed by a fatigue crack, that plane of the main truss would, theoretically, collapse."

This was a steel, arch-truss style bridge with a concrete deck that should have lasted at least 60 years, says P.K. Basu, a civil engineer at Vanderbilt University and an expert on bridge design and failure. Corrosion of rivet connections is a suspect, as are possible cracks around such joints. Some signs of structural failure due to corrosion are subtle, he says, and may only be discernible by experts. Increased weight of trucks in recent years could be another factor.

The bridge was part of Interstate 35, a major transportation link for Minneapolis, and one of the most heavily traveled urban highways in the country. It was also the first of its size in the US to be equipped with an anti-icing system that sprayed a de-icing element on the bridge deck.

President [George W.] Bush on Thursday promised the federal government would respond "robustly" to help with rescue and recovery and with rebuilding the bridge "as quickly as possible." He also blamed Congress for failing to pass crucial spending bills, including funding for infrastructure.

Rep. Jim Oberstar (D) of Minnesota, chairman of the House Transportation and Infrastructure Committee, said Thursday he would ask for $250 million in emergency funding for Minnesota. Some will be used for alternative ways to move 140,000 vehicles a day that used to cross the bridge. Congress had authorized $283 billion for upgrading the nation's infrastructure over five years. Mr. Natale says ASCE felt the figure should have been $360 billion.

9

The Minneapolis Bridge Collapse Was Caused by a Design Flaw

National Transportation Safety Board

The National Transportation Safety Board (NTSB) is an independent US government investigative agency responsible for civil transportation accident investigation.

The I-35W bridge collapse in Minneapolis resulted in seventeen deaths. An investigation showed that the collapse was caused by a design error by the firm that constructed the bridge. This error in the construction of a metal plate uniting structural elements (a gusset plate) was not noticed because gusset plates have not been the focus of evaluation or inspection. Maintenance of the bridge was not at fault, nor was the fact that the bridge was rated as structurally deficient. Rather, the accident was caused by a construction error and by the fact that authorities had not previously focused on the possibility of this kind of deficiency.

About 6:05 p.m. central daylight time on Wednesday, August 1, 2007, the eight-lane, 1,907-foot-long I-35W highway bridge over the Mississippi River in Minneapolis, Minnesota, experienced a catastrophic failure in the main span of the deck truss [structural elements connected to form triangles]. As a result, 1,000 feet of the deck truss collapsed, with about 456 feet of the main span falling 108 feet into the 15-

foot-deep river. A total of 111 vehicles were on the portion of the bridge that collapsed. Of these, 17 were recovered from the water. As a result of the bridge collapse, 13 people died, and 145 people were injured.

Design Error

On the day of the collapse, roadway work was underway on the I-35W bridge, and four of the eight travel lanes (two outside lanes northbound and two inside lanes southbound) were closed to traffic. In the early afternoon, construction equipment and construction aggregates (sand and gravel for making concrete) were delivered and positioned in the two closed inside southbound lanes. The equipment and aggregates, which were being staged for a concrete pour of the southbound lanes that was to begin about 7:00 p.m., were positioned toward the south end of the center section of the deck truss portion of the bridge and were in place by about 2:30 p.m.

The probable cause of the collapse of the I-35W bridge in Minneapolis, Minnesota, was the inadequate load capacity.

About 6:05 p.m., a motion-activated surveillance video camera at the Lower St. Anthony Falls Lock and Dam, just west of the I-35W bridge, recorded a portion of the collapse sequence. The video showed the bridge center span separating from the rest of the bridge and falling into the river.

The National Transportation Safety Board [NTSB] determines that the probable cause of the collapse of the I-35W bridge in Minneapolis, Minnesota, was the inadequate load capacity, due to a design error by Sverdrup & Parcel and Associates, Inc., of the gusset plates [a metal plate used to unite structural members of a truss] at the U10 nodes, which failed under a combination of (1) substantial increases in the weight of the bridge, which resulted from previous bridge modifications, and (2) the traffic and concentrated construction loads on the bridge on the day of the collapse. Contributing to the design error was the failure of Sverdrup & Parcel's quality control procedures to ensure that the appropriate main truss gusset plate calculations were performed for the I-35W bridge and the inadequate design review by Federal and State transportation officials. Contributing to the accident was the generally accepted practice among Federal and State transportation officials of giving inadequate attention to gusset plates during inspections for conditions of distortion, such as bowing, and of excluding gusset plates in load rating analyses.

Before determining that the collapse of the I-35W bridge initiated with failure of the gusset plates at the U10 nodes, the Safety Board considered a number of potential explanations. The following factors were considered, but excluded, as being causal to the collapse: corrosion damage in gusset plates at the L11 nodes, fracture of a floor truss, preexisting cracking, temperature effects, and pier movement.

Safety Issues

The following safety issues were identified in this investigation:

- Insufficient bridge design firm quality control procedures for designing bridges, and insufficient Federal and State procedures for reviewing and approving bridge design plans and calculations.

- Lack of guidance for bridge owners with regard to the placement of construction loads on bridges during repair or maintenance activities.

- Exclusion of gusset plates in bridge load rating guidance.

- Lack of inspection guidance for conditions of gusset plate distortion.

- Inadequate use of technologies for accurately assessing the condition of gusset plates on deck truss bridges.

The inadequate capacity of the U10 node gusset plates had to have been the result of an error on the part of the bridge design firm.

As a result of this accident investigation, the Safety Board makes recommendations to the Federal Highway Administration and the American Association of State Highway and Transportation Officials [AASHTO]. One safety recommendation resulting from this investigation was issued to the Federal Highway Administration in January 2008. . . .

Findings

1. The initiating event in the collapse of the I-35W bridge was a lateral shifting instability of the upper end of the L9/U10W diagonal member and the subsequent failure of the U10 node gusset plates on the center portion of the deck truss.

2. Because the deck truss portion of the I-35W bridge was non-load-path-redundant [that is, it was necessary to bear the load], the total collapse of the deck truss was likely once the gusset plates at the U10 nodes failed.

3. The examination of the collapsed structure, the finite element analysis, and the video recording of the collapse showed that the following were neither causal nor contributory to the collapse of the I-35W bridge: corrosion damage found on the gusset plates at the L11 nodes and elsewhere, fracture of a floor truss, preexisting cracking in the bridge deck truss or approach spans, temperature effects, or shifting of the piers.

4. The initial emergency response to the bridge collapse by fire and rescue units was timely and appropriate, and the incident command system was well coordinated.

5. The damage to bridge components that occurred during victim recovery did not, in this case, prevent determination of the collapse sequence.

6. The gusset plates at the U10 nodes, where the collapse initiated, had inadequate capacity for the expected loads on the structure, even in the original as-designed condition.

7. Because the bridge's main truss gusset plates had been fabricated and installed as the designers specified, the inadequate capacity of the U10 node gusset plates had to have been the result of an error on the part of the bridge design firm.

8. Even though the bridge design firm knew how to correctly calculate the effects of stress in gusset plates, it failed to perform all necessary calculations for the main truss gusset plates of the I-35W bridge, resulting in some of the gusset plates having inadequate capacity, most significantly at the U4 and U4', U10 and U10', and L11 and L11' nodes.

9. Although the U10 gusset plates would have required edge stiffeners according to American Association of State Highway Officials specifications, the addition of stiffeners would not have made the U10 gusset plates adequate or prevented the gusset plates from yielding.

10. The design review process used by the bridge design firm was inadequate in that it did not detect and correct the error in design of the gusset plates at the U4 and U4', U10 and U10', and L11 and L11' nodes before the plans were made final.

11. Neither Federal nor State authorities evaluated the design of the gusset plates for the I-35W bridge in sufficient detail during the design and acceptance process to detect the design errors in the plates, nor was it standard practice for them to do so.

12. Current Federal and State design review procedures are inadequate to detect design errors in bridges.

13. Because current American Association of State Highway and Transportation Officials guidance directs bridge owners to rate their bridges when significant changes occur but not before they place new bridges in service, the load-carrying capacity of new bridges may not be verified before they are opened to traffic.

14. Had American Association of State Highway and Transportation Officials guidance included gusset plates in load ratings, there would have been multiple opportunities to detect the inadequate capacity of the U10 gusset plates of the I-35W bridge deck truss.

15. Because bridge owners generally consider gusset plates to be designed more conservatively than the other members of a truss, because the American Association of State Highway and Transportation Officials provides no specific guidance for the inspection of gusset plates, and because commonly used computer programs for load rating analysis do not include gusset plates, bridge owners typically ignore gusset plates when performing load ratings, and the resulting load ratings might not accurately reflect the actual capacity of the structure.

16. The loading conditions that caused the failure of the improperly designed gusset plates at the U10 nodes included substantial increases in the dead load from bridge modifications and, on the day of the accident, the traffic load and the concentrated loads from the construction materials and equipment; if the gusset plates had been designed in accordance with American Association of State Highway Officials specifications, they would have been able to safely sustain these loads, and the accident would not have occurred.

17. Without clear specifications and guidelines to direct bridge owners regarding the stockpiling of raw materials, they may fail to conduct the appropriate engineering reviews or analyses before permitting raw materials to be stockpiled on a bridge.

18. Although the I-35W bridge had been inspected in accordance with the National Bridge Inspection Standards and more frequently than required by the standards, these inspections would not have been expected to detect design errors.

19. Although the I-35W bridge had been rated under the National Bridge Inspection Standards as *Structurally Deficient* for 16 years before the accident, the conditions responsible for that rating did not cause or contribute to the collapse of the bridge.

20. The bowing of the gusset plates at the U10 and U10' nodes was symptomatic of the inadequate capacity of the plates and occurred under an undetermined load condition before 1999.

21. Because visual bridge inspections alone, regardless of their frequency, are inadequate to always detect corrosion on gusset plates or to accurately assess the extent or progression of that corrosion, inspectors should employ appropriate nondestructive evaluation technologies when evaluating gusset plates.

22. Distortion such as bowing is a sign of an out-of-design condition that should be identified and subjected to further engineering analysis to ensure that the appropriate level of safety is maintained.

23. Because the *AASHTO Guide for Commonly Recognized (CoRe) Structural Elements* does not include gusset plates as a separate bridge inspection element, bridge owners may fail to adequately document and track gusset plate conditions that could threaten the safety of the structure.

24. The lack of specific references to gusset plates in the *Bridge Inspector's Reference Manual* and in National Highway Institute bridge inspector training courses could cause State bridge inspectors during routine or fracture-critical bridge inspections to fail to give appropriate attention to distortions, such as bowing, in gusset plates.

10

The US Government Should Invest More in Mass Transit

Adam Doster and Kate Sheppard

Adam Doster is a senior editor at In These Times, *a nonprofit news magazine, and Kate Sheppard is the political reporter for the online environmental magazine* Grist.

The nation's public transportation system is inadequate. Many people who would like to take public transit cannot do so because there is no infrastructure in place. In addition, public transit is becoming more popular as the environmental consequences of cars become clearer and as the population ages. When polled, the public says that they are willing to invest tax dollars in creating transportation infrastructure. However, in general legislators continue to prefer funding for roads to funding for mass transit. Despite this, roads, too, are underfunded and in need of repair. Federal infrastructure funding priorities and strategies must change to meet public needs.

More than 2.5 million people live in the Baltimore Metropolitan Area and most never step foot on public transit. The city's bus system is slow and inefficient, and the region supports only two rail lines, a 15.5-mile light rail route that traverses the city from north to south and a heavy rail metro track that runs from the city center to the northwestern suburbs. Both lines serve only a combined 80,000 riders daily. Baltimoreans may not prefer driving, but they have little choice.

The Baltimore Rail Plan

That's why local mass transit advocates were thrilled in 2002 when a state advisory committee unveiled the Baltimore Region Rail System Plan, an ambitious proposal that called for the construction of six lines extending more than 109 miles. First on tap was the Red Line, a $1 billion high-capacity east-west rail corridor that would connect with the existing train routes and serve 250,000 people who reside in some of the city's most densely populated but underserved neighborhoods.

"There could be massive economic reinvestment in those areas, which is badly needed," says Stuart Sirota, a regional planner who helped develop the 2002 plan.

> *The United States is a nation of cars. For more than 60 years, federal zoning, housing and transportation policies . . . have diffused the population and established the automobile as the primary means of travel.*

But the project has languished since its inception, stuck under multiyear environmental studies (standard practice for new infrastructure projects), a Republican governor unfriendly to transit expansion and a dearth of federal funds.

By contrast, during the same period, Maryland moved ahead with an equally expensive plan to widen a 10-mile section of I-95, the major interstate that runs along the East Coast. Classified as an upgrade of existing infrastructure, the highway lobby fast-tracked the project—first proposed in 2002—through the environmental regulatory process. Today, it's fully funded and well under construction.

"Transit has been the poor stepchild of highways," says Sirota. "That's been the status quo over the last 40-plus years, and our region isn't any different."

The United States is a nation of cars. For more than 60 years, federal zoning, housing and transportation policies—including President [Dwight] Eisenhower's monumental 1956

Federal-Aid Highway Act—have diffused the population and established the automobile as the primary means of travel.

Prioritizing highway construction over mass transit was justifiable following WWII, when gas was cheap and abundant, climate change [the heating of the earth by fossil fuel emissions] was not yet understood and cities were struggling to handle population growth. Today, it is a recipe for economic and environmental disaster.

Yet the federal government remains in a time warp, prioritizing highway funding even as Americans ditch their cars for seats on trains and buses. This year presents two enormous opportunities to alter the equation: First, the economic recovery package, which will include billions on transit infrastructure, and second, the reauthorization of the surface transportation bill, which could redistribute federal funds.

If bureaucratic inertia and a lack of political imagination don't squash substantive reforms, transportation policy could be fundamentally restructured in 2009. But—especially to judge from the stimulus negotiations—that's a big "if."

Failing Infrastructure

In August 2005, President [George W.] Bush signed into law the current transportation bill—the Safe, Accountable, Flexible, Efficient Transportation Equity Act: A Legacy for Users (SAFETEA-LU)—which will expire Sept. 30, 2009. Infamous for its inclusion of the $200 million "Bridge to Nowhere" [an Alaskan bridge widely derided as unnecessary], the $244 billion bill also failed to improve funding for mass transit.

Since 1982, transportation funding has broken down this way: 80 percent for roads, 20 percent for mass transit. Nothing changed in 2005, leaving Americans with a national mass transit infrastructure that lacks coherent policy vision and desperately needs major investment.

In its 2009 "Report Card for America's Infrastructure Future," the American Society of Civil Engineers (ASCE) gave the United States a "C minus" for its rail network, in part because of the government-owned Amtrak, which the Government Accountability Office recently described as being in "poor financial shape."

And the problems for rail are only worsening: Because freight and intercity passenger trains often share tracks, expected ridership increases will stress an already maxed-out system. ASCE estimates that more than $200 billion is needed through 2035 to accommodate this growth.

ASCE's mark on U.S. mass transit was even worse: a "D." According to the Federal Transit Administration, $15.8 billion is needed annually to maintain conditions of the nation's transit agencies, while improving to "good" conditions would require an annual $21.6 billion. But in 2008, federal funding for transit totaled just $9.8 billion.

Half of all Americans still lack any access to mass transit.

Because funding hasn't kept pace with need, what resources are devoted to mass transit generally cover maintenance and upkeep—not expansion. When Congress reauthorized SAFETEA-LU in 2005, it earmarked a mere $1.6 billion a year for the construction of new commuter and light rail systems, less than 1 percent of the total amount allocated.

"Expenditures are far outpacing revenues," says Deron Lovaas, federal transportation policy director for the Natural Resources Defense Council [NRDC], "and we're not making any improvements."

The pattern creates a staggering backlog. Reconnecting America, which advocates for mass transit, identifies $248 billion in developments that have already been proposed. That's roughly the same amount promised for highways and transit, combined, in the last federal transportation bill. At the current rate of federal investment, it would take 77 years to complete these projects, and that doesn't include the billions of dollars that cities with older systems require to modernize existing transit routes.

Not surprisingly, half of all Americans still lack any access to mass transit, and only 20 percent live near high-capacity outlets (rail or rapid bus), even though 80 percent of Americans reside in areas defined as metropolises.

The Popularity of Transit

Despite deteriorating infrastructure, commuters keep jumping aboard. Since 1995, public transit ridership has risen a whopping 32 percent, more than double the rate of population growth.

In 2007, Americans took 10.3 billion trips on public transportation, the highest number in more than 50 years. The trajectory continued in 2008: Subways, buses, commuter rail and light-rail systems saw a 6.5 percent jump in ridership in the year's third quarter, the largest quarterly upsurge in 25 years.

With transit booming, many Americans are ditching their once-beloved cars. The Federal Highway Administration reports 13 consecutive months of driving decline, with 112 billion less vehicle-miles traveled than in the previous 13-month span.

The high cost of auto transit accounts for some of the behavioral shift. The American Public Transportation Association (APTA), which represents the bus, rapid transit and commuter-rail systems industry, estimates that, by taking transit instead of driving last year, an average household would have saved $9,499, the equivalent of a year's supply of food.

Concern about climate change is also altering transit dynamics. According to APTA, a commuter traveling 20 miles alone by car each day who switches to public transportation would reduce her carbon dioxide emissions by 4,800 pounds per year.

"Americans are driving so much less," says Robert Puentes, a fellow at the Brookings Institution's Metropolitan Policy Program. "But they sure haven't stopped traveling."

Demand for mass transit will only intensify in the future. When Eisenhower launched his grand highway experiment, not only was the U.S. population smaller and younger, but about half of all households were organized as traditional nuclear families—making cars a natural choice upon which to base a transit system.

Not anymore. Today, American households are older (from now until 2030, more people will turn 65 each year than in the previous year), smaller (the share of single person households has edged slightly past the conventional family household) and more attracted to dense, walkable neighborhoods.

"We're not building for an Ozzie-and-Harriet world anymore," says David Goldberg, communications director for Transportation For America (T4), a coalition of more than 100 state and 60 national groups advocating transit reform. "For [moving] goods, for people to get to and from work, for the quality of life in these places, there has to be a well-functioning transportation system that offers a wide range of options."

Republican pollster Frank Luntz recently found that 94 percent of Americans are concerned about the country's infrastructure and 81 percent would be willing to pay 1 percent more on their taxes if the money were to go toward infrastructure. They ranked energy infrastructure as their top priority, but 18 percent listed mass transit as the infrastructure most in need of investment, while passenger rail, bike lanes and pedestrian paths also made it into the top desires.

On Election Day [November 2008], 25 of 33 ballot initiatives to increase local and state taxes for public transportation passed, including an 800-mile high-speed rail line in California that is expected to cost $40 billion by the target completion date in 2030.

"The public sees infrastructure as clean water, they see it as school buildings, they see it as bike paths and airports and railways," Luntz said on a conference call with reporters in December 2008. "They do not just see it as repairing highways."

Having outgrown its current transit system, America must reorganize how its people and its goods move in order to ensure prosperity in the future.

After years of neglect, federal lawmakers are finally taking action. In October, Congress approved a five-year, $13 billion reauthorization of Amtrak, almost double its current federal funding level. Sens. John Kerry (D-Mass.) and Arlen Specter (R-Pa.) followed that up by introducing a law to fund high-speed rail lines in several key corridors of the country. And House members extended tax benefits to bikers and re-established a federal interagency Bicycle Task Force to promote coordination on bike issues.

But these piecemeal reforms pale next to the investments made by other countries. China has opened a new subway system in each of the past six years. And France spends 20 times as much per capita on rail as the United States does.

Having outgrown its current transit system, America must reorganize how its people and its goods move in order to ensure prosperity in the future. An October 2008 American Public Transportation Association survey found that 85 percent of public transit systems reported capacity problems and 35 percent were considering service cuts.

The long-term cost of inaction is even greater. In a January 2008 report authorized by Congress, the National Surface Transportation Policy and Revenue Study Commission concluded that without bold and well-coordinated surface transportation policies, the nation's assets will further deteriorate, greenhouse gas emissions will rise and adverse public health effects will proliferate.

"At the moment, the condition of mass transit is perilous," says T4's Goldberg. "This is a huge turning point."

Roads Hurting Too

The T4 political coalition has grown mightier in recent years. It now includes the American Public Health Association, which sees mass transit and smart-growth as ways to fight health concerns like obesity. And there's talk that the influential American Association of Retired People might sign on as well, pushed by increasing concern that older Americans need mass transit options.

Even funding for roads is hurting these days.

Another notable addition is the National Association of Realtors, which, in the heady days of the McMansion boom, didn't register much concern for mass transit. But as real estate values around transit hubs have exploded, so too has the group's interest.

Defending the status quo will be the American Association of State Highway and Transportation Officials (AASHTO), the umbrella group for state departments of transportation. In years past, legislators have relied heavily on what highway-friendly state transit officials say they need in funding.

AASHTO's highway-heavy stimulus wishlist is a prime example. Florida devoted only 1 percent of its $6.97 billion request to mass transit; Missouri around 5 percent of its $800 million request. Even more progressive transit-policy states, such as California and New York, asked for less than half of their funding to go to transit.

Road builders and others from the concrete lobby, like the American Road and Transportation Builders Association (ARTBA), will also weigh in. AASHTO and ARTBA have sway in Congress, going back to the days when the country's interstates were a major source of jobs. For 27 years, these groups have preserved their lopsided funding allotment.

But even funding for roads is hurting these days. In September 2008, the Federal Highway Trust Fund—which uses the gas tax to fund a majority of road repair projects—went broke, forcing Congress to spend $8 billion to ensure temporary solvency. Yet the fund is expected to run out again later this year, leading even the most conservative transit policy-makers to talk about greener options.

Some in Congress are lobbying for a simple gas tax increase to fix the highway-funding problem. But that idea doesn't take into account that gasoline-powered cars are becoming increasingly fuel-efficient, much less that battery, bio-fuel and plug-in hybrid technologies have begun to permeate the market.

Another idea is for a mileage tax. Several states are now considering it, and Portland, Ore., already tried it in 2006 and 2007. Cars were equipped with a mileage counter, and when they filled up at fuel stations, they were levied a tax for the number of miles they had traveled, rather than charged a gas tax at the pump. It was fairly popular with testers—91 percent of participants liked it more than the gas tax, according to survey by the Oregon Department of Transportation—but the program is not ready to scale nationally.

But to reshape policy, NRDC's Lovaas says one method could be to specify that money meant for highway and bridge projects be used only for repair and maintenance. Another policy proposal would include language specifying that repair projects be given priority over new road construction when funding is distributed.

Others are focusing on the percentages: While transit advocates would ideally like a 50-50 split between roads and mass transit funding, T4 is lobbying for a 60-40 split, which would still increase funding for mass transit from its current level.

Transit advocates will likely differ over just how far to go in advocating for a better apportionment. Friends of the Earth (FOE) launched a "no new roads" campaign around the stimulus plan, calling instead for cleaner alternatives.

But others, like the Congress for the New Urbanism (CNU), don't necessarily oppose new roads. They only oppose roads and projects that don't address congestion, sprawl and inaccessibility.

"In the past, the environmental movement and the smart growth movement have sort of just juxtaposed roads to mass transit," says CNU President and former Milwaukee Mayor John Norquist. He argues that road funding should instead be based on whether it creates a network of accessible, user-friendly streets for pedestrians, mass transit and cars.

A Less-than-Stimulating Start

Meanwhile, House Transportation and Infrastructure Committee Chair James Oberstar (D-Minn.)—who will likely have plenty of say in what the House transit package looks like—has sent signals that he'll fight for something tougher than previous transportation bills. His original stimulus proposal called for $85 billion for infrastructure investments, with more than half going to energy and environmental projects and at least $17 billion to mass transit. Of that, $12 billion would go to public transit, and $5 billion for rail. Another $30 billion would go to highways and bridges. Oberstar noted that his plan "creates green-collar jobs and invests in projects that decrease our dependence on foreign oil and address global climate change."

However, when the stimulus proposal came out in mid-January [2009], the road money stayed the same but the transportation portion had been reduced by 25 percent. As for rail—for which Oberstar wanted $5 billion—its funding was reduced to $1.1 billion. Transit advocates were able to tack $3 billion more onto the stimulus through an amendment, but the total was still short of what Oberstar originally called for.

"How those decisions were made, I don't know," says Jim Berard, communications director for the House Transportation and Infrastructure Committee. "It's disappointing that our recommendation was not accepted on the whole, but at the same time we got a good deal for transportation infrastructure and we want to keep the momentum going for this bill."

The Senate Appropriations Committee's draft stimulus was even more meager than the House version, providing just $9.5 billion for transit. The chamber then rejected an amendment offered by Sens. Patty Murray (D-Wash.) and Dianne Feinstein (D-Calif.) to increase transportation funding by $18 billion—$5 billion for mass transit and $13 billion for highways—by a mere two votes. Instead, lawmakers tacked on an additional $11.5 billion in tax rebates for car purchases, forcing struggling local transit agencies to shore up their riddled budgets in-house.

At least $50 billion worth of backlogged repairs are needed for public transit systems, compared to $8.5 billion needed to maintain current roads.

And as *In These Times* went to press [February 2009] Sen. Barbara Boxer (D-Calif.), chair of the Environment and Public Works Committee, was reportedly co-sponsoring an amendment with notorious climate change skeptic Sen. James Inhofe (R-Okla.) that would throw an additional $50 billion at roads and highways. As Boxer's committee will be responsible for the reauthorization of the transporation bill, the amendment doesn't bode well.

"It shows that there's absolutely no new thinking coming out of that committee on the role that transportation needs to play in achieving global warming goals," says FOE's Transportaion Coordinator Colin Peppard. "We need better leadership from the committee that's going to be drafting this bill."

Those who favor spending on roads argue that they provide a more immediate stimulus because they're "shovel-ready." But at least $50 billion worth of backlogged repairs are needed for public transit systems, compared to $8.5 billion needed to maintain current roads. Yet the stimulus draft gave billions more to roads—meaning much would likely be spent on expanding or building new roads.

Meanwhile, despite the fact that Amtrak's northeast corridor alone needs more than $10 billion in repairs, the draft allocated only $1.1 billion for improving all of Amtrak. Yet even this pittance was deemed too generous by Sens. Ben Nelson (D-Neb.) and Susan Collins (R-Maine), who, as *In These Times* went to press, had proposed slashing it by $850 million.

Berard, however, remains bullish about the coming congressional session. "There will be other times down the road to advocate for more transit funding," he says. "We will be taking a very close look at how to get more for transit in that as well."

Though unable to give a sense of dollar figures or percentages, Berard says the preliminary work on the legislation is underway, and legislators plan to move a bill through the House by the end of June.

11

The United States Must Invest in New Technologies Like High-Speed Rail

Jesse Lee

Jesse Lee is the director of the White House Progressive Media & Online Response.

High-speed rail has helped transform transportation and spur economic activity in many nations, including France and China. So far, the United States has not invested in high-speed rail, but that is going to change with President Barack Obama's new strategic plan. In addition to its other benefits, high-speed rail will also lower American dependence on foreign oil, reduce traffic congestion, and help the environment by reducing greenhouse gas emissions.

"I'm happy to be here. I'm more happy than you can imagine," said the Vice President [Joe Biden], a noted rail enthusiast, before introducing the President [Barack Obama] for the release of his strategic plan, for high speed rail in America. Revolving around the $8 billion in the Recovery Act and the $1 billion per year for five years requested in the President's budget to get these projects off the ground, the President painted the picture that will become a reality as a result of these investments:

> What we're talking about is a vision for high-speed rail in America. Imagine boarding a train in the center of a city. No racing to an airport and across a terminal, no delays, no

sitting on the tarmac, no lost luggage, no taking off your shoes. (Laughter.) Imagine whisking through towns at speeds over 100 miles an hour, walking only a few steps to public transportation, and ending up just blocks from your destination. Imagine what a great project that would be to rebuild America.

Now, all of you know this is not some fanciful, pie-in-the-sky vision of the future. It is now. It is happening right now. It's been happening for decades. The problem is it's been happening elsewhere, not here.

In France, high-speed rail has pulled regions from isolation, ignited growth, remade quiet towns into thriving tourist destinations. In Spain, a high-speed line between Madrid and Seville is so successful that more people travel between those cities by rail than by car and airplane combined. China, where service began just two years ago, may have more miles of high-speed rail service than any other country just five years from now. And Japan, the nation that unveiled the first high-speed rail system, is already at work building the next: a line that will connect Tokyo with Osaka at speeds of over 300 miles per hour. So it's being done; it's just not being done here.

There's no reason why we can't do this. This is America. There's no reason why the future of travel should lie somewhere else beyond our borders. Building a new system of high-speed rail in America will be faster, cheaper and easier than building more freeways or adding to an already overburdened aviation system—and everybody stands to benefit.

With high-speed rail system, we're going to be able to pull people off the road, lowering our dependence on foreign oil, lowering the bill for our gas in our gas tanks.

The inclusion of high speed rail in the Recovery Act was one of many symbols of the new vision for America and its economy that guided the plan. As the Vice President explained in his introduction, joined by Transportation Secretary [Ray] LaHood, in addition to putting Americans to work across the country it went towards several of the Recovery Act's key goals:

> And we're making a down payment today, a down payment on the economy for tomorrow, the economy that's going to drive us in the 21st century in a way that the other—the highway system—drove us in the mid-20th century. And I'm happy to be here. I'm more happy than you can imagine—(laughter)—to talk about a commitment that, with the President's leadership, we're making to achieve the goal through the development of high-speed rail projects that will extend eventually all across this nation. And most of you know that not only means an awful lot to me, but I know a lot of you personally in this audience over the years, I know it means equally as much to you.
>
> With high-speed rail system, we're going to be able to pull people off the road, lowering our dependence on foreign oil, lowering the bill for our gas in our gas tanks. We're going to loosen the congestion that also has great impact on productivity, I might add, the people sitting at stop lights right now in overcrowded streets and cities. We're also going to deal with the suffocation that's taking place in our major metropolitan areas as a consequence of that congestion. And we're going to significantly lessen the damage to our planet. This is a giant environmental down payment.

12

The Federal Government Should Not Invest in High-Speed Rail

Dave Bohon

Dave Bohon is a writer for The New American.

The Barack Obama Administration is proposing massive spending on high-speed rail, claiming that this would make the United States more globally competitive. However, rail investment in America has never worked. The Amtrak rail system has never turned a profit and has required ongoing large federal investment to continue operating. Similarly, high-speed rail would not attract enough users from cars and planes to be economically viable. Worst of all, the plan to spend money on high-speed rail is a government plan to force people out of their cars and into trains, changing the way Americans travel.

On February 8 [2011] Vice President Joe Biden unveiled an [Barack] Obama administration plan to spend $53 billion over the next six years to develop a high-speed passenger rail system that would link the nation's larger cities. The proposed spending would be added to the $10.5 billion the administration has already spent on high-speed rail since Obama took office, including $8 billion poured into his 2009 "economic stimulus package."

Dave Bohon, "Obama Administration Proposes $53 Billion for High-Speed Rail," *New American* online, February 15, 2011. TheNewAmerican.com. Copyright © 2011 by The New American. All rights reserved. Reproduced by permission.

More Money for Rail

The proposed new plan would include $8 billion in spending on the project in the upcoming fiscal year, and would feature an application process to streamline how cities, states, and private investors would tap into federal tax dollars to "partner" with the federal government in developing the nationwide high-speed rail system.

"There are key places where we cannot afford to sacrifice as a nation—one of which is infrastructure," Biden, a long-time advocate of high-speed rail, declared as he introduced the plan. He emphasized the crucial need "to invest in a modern rail system that will help connect communities, reduce congestion, and create quality, skilled manufacturing jobs that cannot be outsourced."

With both government and private concerns relying heavily on automobiles over the past 60 years, America's rail system has not been a high priority for either sector.

The Vice President's announcement followed the President's own declaration during his January 25 [2011] State of the Union address that high-speed rail is a key element of the nation's economic recovery. "To attract new businesses to our shores, we need the fastest, most reliable ways to move people, goods, and information—from high-speed rail to high-speed Internet," Obama told Congress and the American people. "Countries in Europe and Russia invest more in their roads and railways than we do. China is building faster trains and newer airports."

The President said his proposal would extend rail service to the nation's largest urban areas and give an estimated 80 percent of Americans access to the service within the next 25 years. "This could allow you to go places in half the time it takes to travel by car," he said. "For some trips, it will be faster than flying—without the pat-down."

With both government and private concerns relying heavily on automobiles over the past 60 years, America's rail system has not been a high priority for either sector. Writing on Time.com, Bryan Walsh noted that "America's antiquated rail system will have to advance a long way just to make it to the present, let alone the future. U.S. intercity railroads are a laughingstock compared with those in most other developed nations—and, increasingly, even those in developing nations like China, which is investing more than $300 billion to build more than 16,000 miles of high-speed track by 2020."

> *Republicans . . . point out that with a record $14 trillion federal debt, ratcheting up federal spending on such a dubious program as America's traditionally-failed passenger rail system doesn't make sense.*

The proposal that Biden laid out calls for spending up to $500 billion over the next 25 years to remedy this supposed defect, with plans for a system that would include regional corridors with trains traveling at speeds of 90 to 125 mph, along with a faster express rail system that would form the foundation for a high-speed system with electric trains traveling at speeds of 125 to 250 mph.

Republicans Opposed

But Republicans in both the House and the Senate point out that with a record $14 trillion federal debt, ratcheting up federal spending on such a dubious program as America's traditionally-failed passenger rail system doesn't make sense. In fact, legislators studying the issue said that ending rail subsidies now would trim as much as $6 billion from the budget.

U.S. Representative John Mica (R-Fla.), chairman of the House Transportation and Infrastructure Committee and a proponent of improving the nation's rail system, condemned the President's plan, part of which would be used to speed up trains in the nation's most heavily traveled rail corridor, the Amtrak-run Boston-New York-Washington route, reported the AFP news service. "Amtrak's Soviet-style train system is not the way to provide modern and efficient passenger rail service," observed Mica, who has proposed that such projects should be financed and operated privately.

Representative Bill Shuster (R-Pa.), chairman of the Railroads subcommittee, joined Mica in criticizing the Obama administration's plan, arguing that it fails to attract "private investment, capital, and the experience to properly develop and cost-effectively operate true high-speed rail." Noting the long-term failure of federally subsidized Amtrak, Shuster said that the "definition of insanity is doing the same thing over and over again, expecting a different result, and that is exactly what Vice President Biden offered today."

Shuster said that the only sound model for successful high-speed rail in the U.S. would be one that is funded and operated by private investors. "Rail projects that are not economically sound will not win the future," he said. "It just prolongs the inevitable by subsidizing a failed Amtrak monopoly that has never made a profit or even broken even. Government won't develop American high-speed rail. Private investment and a competitive market will."

In a *Washington Post* editorial, Robert Samuelson suggested that the President's proposal casts doubt on his stated commitment to reduce the budget deficit. Samuelson wondered how Obama's proposed $3.73 trillion budget, in which he promises to cut spending by $1.1 trillion, will "subdue deficits if it keeps proposing big spending programs?"

Samuelson noted that when Congress created Amtrak in 1970 "to preserve intercity passenger trains, the idea was that the system would become profitable and self-sustaining after an initial infusion of federal money. This never happened. Amtrak has swallowed $35 billion in subsidies, and they're increasing by more than $1 billion annually."

Despite the hefty government subsidies, wrote Samuelson, Amtrak travel is no bargain for travelers, with a recent one-way trip from Washington, D.C. to New York City going for $139—compared to a $21.50 round-trip fare by private bus service. "Nor does Amtrak do much to relieve congestion, cut oil use, reduce pollution or eliminate greenhouse gases," he added, addressing the arguments advanced by environmentalists for subsidized rail service. "Its traffic volumes are simply too small to matter." Samuelson recalled that last year Amtrak carried a meager 29.1 million passengers—about four percent of the estimated 725 million passengers who flew by air during the same period, and about 25 percent of the 124 million Americans who commute by automobile each day. "Measured by passenger-miles traveled, Amtrak represents one-tenth of 1 percent of the national total," he said.

What's disheartening about the Obama administration's embrace of high-speed rail is that it ignores history, evidence and logic.

As in the past with federally subsidized rail, once the dust settles and the bill comes due for construction and equipment (not to mention maintenance and repairs), in order to recoup costs operators would be forced to raise ticket prices so high that few would choose it as an option. By contrast, while lowering prices might increase ridership, the increased revenue would not begin to cover costs. Literally all government-run mass transit systems run in the red, and Obama's white elephant dream would be no exception.

The Overwhelming Case Against Rail Service

"The reasons passenger rail service doesn't work in America are well-known," noted Samuelson. "Interstate highways shorten many trip times; suburbanization has fragmented destination points; air travel is quicker and more flexible for long distances. . . . Against history and logic is the imagery of high-speed rail as 'green' and a cutting-edge technology."

While Samuelson is clearly a proponent of big government, which he says exists to make "wise choices" for us all, his observations on a federalized high-speed rail system are sound as far as they go. "What's disheartening about the Obama administration's embrace of high-speed rail is that it ignores history, evidence and logic," he wrote. "The case against it is overwhelming. The case in favor rests on fashionable platitudes. High-speed rail is not an 'investment in the future'; it's mostly a waste of money."

One of the missing points in Samuelson's editorial, as well as other discussions on the issue, is the pressure that would likely come from environmentalists and others, should a federalized rail service move forward, to take private vehicles out of the hands of Americans—essentially making them too expensive to own—and force them to use alternative forms of transportation from walking and bicycles to buses and cramped trains.

Time magazine's Bryan Walsh cited statistics from the activist group Environment America which supposedly shows that high-speed rail uses a third less energy per mile than auto or air travel, and a nationwide system could even reduce the nation's oil consumption by 125 million barrels a year. "In addition, high-speed rail represents the kind of long-term infrastructure investment that will pay back for decades, just as the interstate highway system of the 1950s has," wrote Walsh, suggesting an eventual segue from cars to trains as America's main mode of long-distance transportation.

Perhaps Biden himself was offering a federally-inspired prophetic look at America's future when he called the proposed rail system "a down payment on a truly national program" that would "change the way we travel and change the way we work and live."

13

The United States Must Create New Systems That Promote Sustainability

Diana Lind

Diana Lind is an urban advocate, a writer, and the executive director and editor-in-chief of the magazine Next American City.

Electric cars are a way to reduce carbon emissions and address some environmental concerns. However, they are only a small step, when what is really needed is sweeping change. Cars, even electric ones, contribute to sprawl and are ultimately powered by fossil fuels, since most electric plants, which provide electricity to charge the cars, rely on coal. What is really needed is a decisive move away from cars and towards more sustainable forms of transit in cities. Urban areas should focus on bicycles, trains, and public transit, perhaps even banning cars from downtowns.

Who wants to argue against the positive impacts of small steps toward sustainability? I don't—but I have to.

There's no doubt that small efforts are meaningful. Using compact fluorescent light bulbs instead of incandescent ones lowers humanity's carbon footprint. Recycling instead of throwing away plastic and paper saves acres of trash from landfills, and using plant-based detergents instead of harsh chemicals keeps harmful toxics out of our ecosystems. But taking a long view, these are minor ways to counter monumental climate change and the degradation of our natural environment.

Think Big

What if, instead of promoting slight modifications to our behavior, we created new systems that led us on a radical path toward sustainability? What if, instead of promoting recycling, we taxed disposable items that could not be reused, making a plastic bottle of water cost $5 instead of $1? Think about how many bottles of water would never be purchased and instead how much more urgently the public would fight for clean tap water.

There are countless ways we could rethink our consumption and our carbon-fueled behavior, but instead we rally around "smarter" choices—compact fluorescent bulbs and recycling plastic, for example—that merely delay, rather than prevent, inevitable environmental catastrophe. Case in point: the move toward electric cars and the investment in new car infrastructure to accommodate these new vehicles.

What if cities outlawed private cars for leisure purposes?

Sure, electric cars may offer an improvement upon gas-fueled cars, but this innovation is insufficient to create the kind of social, economic, and environmental sustainability our planet needs. You'll hear electric car advocates praise the fact that hybrids can be fueled by solar and wind energy, rather than coal-sourced electricity. But recent estimates show that solar, wind, and geothermal energy account for only about 7 percent of the world's total energy. While I am hopeful that one day our country will run on renewable energy, it is naive to assume that the country's 250 million vehicles would, if plugged in anytime soon, be fueled by anything other than coal. That's the very same coal whose high carbon emissions are guaranteed to push us past the ecological tipping point.

In any case, changing the source of a car's fuel does not change the fact that the car still contributes to a number of other major environmental and socio-economic problems. To name just a few: Cars fuel sprawl, create hideous hours-long commutes, contribute to the obesity epidemic, and are accomplices to our ever-worsening social isolation. Consider the fact that car-oriented communities are much less sustainable than walkable communities. For example, our auto-dependent suburbs and exurbs typically are zoned for larger houses and bigger commercial spaces, all of which consume much more energy than compact, dense cities.

Cities Are Key

If you then agree that cities are the key to sustainability, then mayors and transportation directors shouldn't be encouraging car usage. As Dean Kamen, the creator of the Segway, will tell you, cars move at a speed of about eight miles per hour in cities—they actually aren't suited to the fast pace of urban places. Bikes, buses, and subways move much quicker and provide the public with a variety of other benefits—from the health benefits of biking to the economic benefits of inexpensive public transportation. Will cars ever really be "plug-in-and-play?" I don't think so. And I fear cash-strapped cities are going to end up with a new kind of electric bill—the kind that pays for new infrastructure to service electric cars, at a time when economic strains should be encouraging greater public transit.

We are fortunate to live at a time when all major municipalities are serious about sustainability. But shouldn't the advent of the electric car provide a perfect moment to rethink how cities incorporate cars in their urban fabric? Instead of creating new electric car plug-in infrastructure, which will undoubtedly become outdated within a decade or two, is it not time to rethink personal mobility altogether? What if cities outlawed private cars for leisure purposes? What if money otherwise spent on plug-in infrastructure went toward feasibility studies for car-free downtown centers?

Anyone who thinks that this kind of transformation in cities is beyond our capability for change should remember this: We once ripped up public transportation infrastructure and built highways through our downtowns. It is no more outlandish to think that we could reverse these changes today if we created comprehensive plans to wean cities off cars. Wouldn't that be smarter?

14

The Federal Government Must Reexamine Transportation Spending

Ben Adler

Ben Adler has been a staff writer at Politico *and an editor at* Newsweek *and* The Center for American Progress.

The current system for transportation funding in the United States is broken. America mostly relies on gas taxes to fund roads, but gas tax revenues are falling as people move to more efficient vehicles and drive less. Republicans in Congress are unwilling to institute other taxes to make up the shortfall. In addition, they are reluctant to fund mass transit systems, and they refuse to engage in thoughtful transportation planning. For example, Republicans do not allow local jurisdictions to institute tolls on federal highways and are doing little to encourage private/public partnerships. As a result, transportation policy is irrational and ineffective.

When Representative John Mica, a Republican from Florida and chair of the House Transportation Committee released his proposal for the overdue Surface Transportation Reauthorization bill earlier this month [July 2011], liberals condemned the plan's lack of investment in infrastructure. They missed, however, a bigger failing: Transportation spending is not just underfunded in this country; it's broken, and we can't afford to wait another six years to fix it. House Republicans, though, haven't proposed sensible transportation policy changes, even ones conservatives should support.

No New Taxes

Smart-growth advocates, unions, and environmentalists had been excited by President Barack Obama's $556 billion proposal for the six-year transportation bill, but Mica's plan offers a mere $230 billion because Republicans are unwilling to raise the gasoline tax, which pays for federal transportation spending. They are also unwilling to create new sources of funding such as a tax on vehicle miles traveled (this would be achieved using GPS [global positioning system] monitoring). But gasoline-tax revenues are actually declining, not just holding steady, because of lower usage during the recession and increasing vehicle efficiency. Whereas President George W. Bush was happy to cover the shortfall between gas-tax revenues and authorized transportation spending by taking money from general funds, these newly principled Republicans won't do that. So per-year spending on transportation would decline from $52 billion to $35 billion per year when it should be going up to meet our growing needs.

The commitment to squeezing domestic discretionary spending, however, is more important to House Republicans. Mica actually supports raising funds for transportation—he co-sponsored a much larger proposal with former Chair Jim Oberstar last year—but he cannot get Republican support for it in the current environment. "He's collared by the fact that the [Congressman Paul] Ryan budget only allows this much money for [transportation]," says David Burwell, author of a recently released comprehensive report on surface transportation reauthorization from the Carnegie Endowment.

Senator Barbara Boxer, a Democrat from California who chairs the Environment and Public Works Committee, may introduce a two-year extension that would implement reforms while we wait for the economic and political circumstances for raising the gas tax to improve. But House Republicans are going a different route, proposing a full six-year extension that leaves out many of the performance and accountability standards we should adopt. For a party that talks a good game about improving efficiency in government programs, the GOP sure isn't acting like it.

The truth is that there was little political appetite for a gasoline-tax increase before Republicans took control of the House and, going into an election year, there is none today. The Obama administration has repeatedly poured cold water on rumors that officials were secretly working on a gasoline-tax increase or vehicle-miles-traveled proposal.

But transportation wonks and the Obama administration have a whole list of reforms to include in the transportation reauthorization, which could spend the money we do have more effectively. Most of the proposals floating around in the think-tank world involve bringing the kind of business best practices to federal transportation spending that Republicans claim to love. Most of them have been left out of Mica's proposal.

The Federal Government Should Set Goals

Currently, the federal government passes money to states and localities for transportation projects without metrics on what should be achieved. Instead, we should set goals for our transportation policy, such as reducing carbon emissions and dependence on oil, measure whether projects have helped us to meet them, and hold states accountable. The Republican proposal, though, says that formulas will determine 90 percent of funding. You can't hold states accountable if you can't withhold their money. Nor is it even clear what goals we would measure progress against.

"Right now, there is no purpose to the program," explains Robert Puentes, a transportation expert at the Brookings Institution. "Money comes into the federal government and goes out based on public support. It should have an objective, such as bridge repair or reducing carbon emissions, and then choose on that basis and measure success at it."

Providing transportation choices, rather than deciding in Washington that everyone should drive, and foisting that decision on citizens through federal spending that favors roads, is hardly a conservative principle.

Mica's proposal also did not address how American highways have scarred our landscape and made us dependent on cars. It's not a given that large roads can't accommodate pedestrians and bicycles. Urban boulevards from before the mid-20th century have tree-lined sidewalks, bike lanes, and street parking. They work within the street grid and enhance, rather than destroy, neighborhoods. But our federally subsidized highways have generally made no accommodations for other modes of travel. To make matters worse, Mica's bill would eliminate the 1 percent of transportation spending currently set aside to help communities build bicycle or pedestrian paths.

Mass transit will fair poorly, too. By cutting funding without adjusting the traditional 80/20 formula for roads and mass transit, new projects are almost certain not to get federal support. "It's pretty bad news for transit," says David Goldberg, communications director at Transportation for America. "The Mica bill puts emphasis on formula grants to transit agencies, almost to the exclusion of project funding. There's a bunch of projects in the pipeline now, the new starts program is oversubscribed as it is, and communities are waiting in line. With less money, the waits would be even longer. Pretty much anything new seeking federal funds would be out of luck."

Providing transportation choices, rather than deciding in Washington that everyone should drive, and foisting that decision on citizens through federal spending that favors roads, is hardly a conservative principle. The conservative principle of disinvestment, though, is more important to many Republicans. As Goldberg notes, "It could have been worse. There were some in Mica's caucus who would have eliminated transit altogether."

Private-Public Partnerships

Another tactic that Republicans should embrace is private-public partnerships. In certain areas, such as suburban Virginia, business owners have seen the benefits of extended mass transit and have volunteered to help fund construction of stations near them. This, though, happens on only a local and ad-hoc basis. While the Republican proposal contains some hand-waving language regarding private-public partnerships, considerable investment in such strategies won't happen without a plan to leverage them in appropriate ways in different places. Creating a national infrastructure bank to manage and provide seed money for these projects is a good idea that Obama proposed but Mica has not.

Finally, for supposed advocates of local control and the magic of the market, House Republicans have failed to promote either adequately when it comes to transportation. Take congestion pricing: Currently, states are not allowed to put tolls on their section of an Interstate highway. But the best way to unclog highways would be with tolling at high-volume times or for single-occupancy vehicles. Some states would do this if given the freedom. Yet Republicans have not proposed letting local governments harness the market's ability to price a good more effectively.

To be fair, the Republicans' bill contains bright spots. The GOP [Republican party] would streamline the bureaucracy by combining or eliminating outdated programs, although experts caution that the devil will be in the still-unannounced details. States will be allowed to add tolls to non-Interstate highways that receive federal funding and to toll new lanes on Interstates. Overall, however, the Republicans' resistance to spending money, or even spending it wisely, means we will continue to fall behind other countries when it comes to building our transportation infrastructure.

15

Tolls and Private Investment Should Fund Infrastructure Improvement

Emily Ekins

Emily Ekins is a research fellow at the Cato Institute, a public policy research organization in Washington, DC.

A recent poll shows that the public prefers to fund most transportation projects through public-private partnerships, and believes high-speed rail should be funded through private companies. The poll also shows that people oppose raising the federal gas tax, and would prefer to pay for roads through tolls. The poll suggests that the federal government should let private companies fund train transit and should move away from the gas tax in favor of tolls on roads.

With states bringing in lower tax revenues, strapped budgets, and increasing transportation usage, governments are looking to partner with private firms to provide transportation improvements and expansions. According to the recent Reason-Rupe poll, 55% of Americans favor these kinds of partnerships. In fact, a majority of all political groups favor government working with private companies to further transportation projects.

Public Opinion Favors Private High-Speed Rail

When Americans are asked to choose between government and private business building high-speed rail, however, a majority of Americans (55 percent) want private enterprise to build this infrastructure.

In contrast, 34 percent believe government should build high-speed rail. Partisan divisions do arise for this issue of high-speed rail: a plurality of Democrats and Occupy Wall Street supporters prefer government build with taxpayer money, however a majority of pure Independents, Tea Party Supporters and Republicans prefer private companies to build these railways.

A partial driver of partisan division may be that if governments were to build high-speed railways, they would build where policymakers think they are needed; in contrast, private businesses would build railways where it is profitable to build—so where a substantial number of riders would pay to use them. In sum, deciding between public or private building of high-speed rail contrasts goals of efficiency and access, and political groups make trade-offs between efficiency and access differently.

If this poll has accurately gauged attitudes toward government or private enterprise building and operating railway infrastructure, this casts doubt on how Amtrak [the government rail system] is currently run. Currently, many Amtrak lines operate at a loss because policymakers often choose access to rail lines over efficiency in running the trains, even in areas where there is little demand for train use.

Funding Roads with Tolls, Not Taxes

As the number of people using roads and highways steadily increases, cars have also become more fuel-efficient, thus reducing the amount of gas purchased per person. This is good news for consumers; however, transportation spending is largely funded from gasoline taxes, and those receipts are decreasing. The recent Reason-Rupe poll asked Americans how they would prefer to fund transit going forward.

Governments are failing to meet demand for toll roads while focusing efforts on other ways to raise revenue and reduce congestion.

Policymakers have considered increasing the federal gas tax, currently 18.4 cents per gallon in efforts to close the spending-funding gap. Yet 77 percent of Americans oppose raising the federal gas tax. Part of the aversion may be a concern that the government will not spend the tax dollars effectively—65 percent of Americans think the government generally spends transportation funding ineffectively.

Rather than tax increases, the poll found that 58 percent prefer paying for new roads and highways by paying tolls when they drive on the roads. Interestingly, another 58 percent of Americans also report there are not toll roads in their area, but 59 percent say they would pay to use a toll lane if governments constructed them and if these lanes would save them time in traffic. This indicates governments are failing to meet demand for toll roads while focusing efforts on other ways to raise revenue and reduce congestion. These findings suggest that policymakers' attention may need to shift to meet demand for toll roads.

Governments are also considering partnering with private companies to build and expand highways, airports, and other infrastructure projects that they might not be able to afford without the efficiency and expertise of the private sector. Thus in addition to raising revenues, governments are also seeking opportunities to reduce costs for roads. However, some are uneasy with private companies building and operating transportation, as they believe this is a role for government. Nevertheless, 55 percent of Americans favor private-public partnerships while 35 percent oppose.

Another opportunity to raise revenue and potentially reduce congestion is to open high occupancy vehicle lanes (HOV), previously reserved for carpools, to single drivers who pay a toll. Some point out that this not only can raise revenue, but also offer drivers a faster trip when they need it. However, others point out that lower-income families would be less able or willing to pay the tolls, making this policy unfair. The Reason-Rupe poll found that 57 percent favor opening HOV lanes to toll-paying drivers and 35 percent oppose.

Another plan governments are considering is to charge adjustable tolls on new toll roads and lanes. Instead of charging the same fee, the tolls would be higher during rush hours and lower when traffic is light. However, 50 percent of Americans oppose this proposal and 39 percent favor it.

Organizations to Contact

The editors have compiled the following list of organizations concerned with the issues debated in this book. The descriptions are derived from materials provided by the organizations. All have publications or information available for interested readers. The list was compiled on the date of publication of the present volume; the information provided here may change. Be aware that many organizations take several weeks or longer to respond to inquiries, so allow as much time as possible.

American Association of State Highway and Transportation Officials (AASHTO)
444 N Capitol St. NW, Suite 249, Washington, DC   20001
(202) 624-5800 • fax: (202) 624-5806
e-mail: info@aashto.org
website: www.transportation.org

AASHTO represents state highway departments and advocates transportation polices that support state efforts to promote safe and efficient highway transportation. It publishes the weekly *AASHTO Journal*, reports, and press releases on transportation issues. The ASSHTO website includes recent news and excerpts from its publications, including "AASHTO Statement on Proposed National Highway System Bridge Reconstruction Initiative."

American Public Works Association (APWA)
1275 K St. NW, Suite 750, Washington, DC   20005
(202) 408-9541 • fax: (202) 408-9542
website: www.apwa.net

APWA is an association of public agencies, private sector companies, and individuals whose mission is to provide high quality public works. Its publications, including the monthly *APWA Reporter*, provide information and analysis on infrastructure-related public policy. Recent issues of the *APWA Reporter* are available on the organization's website.

American Society of Civil Engineers (ASCE)
1801 Alexander Bell Dr., Reston, VA   20191
(800) 548-2723
website: www.asce.org

ASCE is a professional organization for civil engineers. It is dedicated to advancing technology, encouraging lifelong learning, promoting professionalism, developing civil engineering leaders, and advocating infrastructure and environmental stewardship. Its website includes numerous resources, reports, and multimedia presentations, including "2009 Report Card for America's Infrastructure" and *The Vision for Civil Engineering in 2025.*

Brookings Institution
1775 Massachusetts Ave. NW, Washington, DC   20036-2188
(202) 797-6000
e-mail: communications@brookings.edu
website: www.brookings.edu

The Brookings Institution is a liberal think tank that conducts research and education in foreign policy, economics, government, and the social sciences. It publishes the quarterly *Brookings Review*, the biannual *Brookings Papers on Economic Activity*, and various books. Its website includes articles and videos such as "Investing in Transportation Infrastructure: A Live Web Chat with Robert Puentes" and "Transformative Investments in Infrastructure, Chicago Style."

Cato Institute
1000 Massachusetts Ave. NW, Washington, DC   20001-5403
(202) 842-0200 • fax: (202) 842-3490
website: www.cato.org

The Cato Institute is a libertarian public policy research organization dedicated to increasing the understanding of public policies based on the principles of limited government, free markets, individual liberty, and peace. It publishes the triannual *Cato Journal*, the periodic *Cato Policy Analysis*, and a bimonthly newsletter, *Cato Policy Review*. Its website also includes multimedia presentations and such articles as "Infrastructure Projects to Fix the Economy? Don't Bank on It" and "Federal Infrastructure Spending: How About This Boondoggle."

Center for American Progress
1333 H St. NW, 10th Floor, Washington, DC   20005
(202) 682-1611 • fax: (202) 682-1867
e-mail: progress@americanprogress.org
website: www.americanprogress.org

The Center for American Progress is a progressive think tank with an interest in values like diversity, shared and personal responsibility, and participatory government. It publishes broadly on economic issues including business and regulation, credit and debt, the global economy, health care, immigration, and the environment. Its website includes articles and reports such as "Meeting the Infrastructure Imperative" and "Idea of the Day: Boosting Infrastructure Investments Generates Business, Creates Jobs, and Boosts Public Safety."

Economic Policy Institute
1333 H St. NW, Suite 300, East Tower
Washington, DC   20005-4707
(202) 775-8810 • fax: (202) 775-0819
e-mail: researchdept@epi.org
website: www.epi.org

The Economic Policy Institute is a nonprofit think tank that focuses on the economic policy interests of low- and middle-income workers. It conducts research, publishes studies and books, briefs policymakers, provides support to activists, and provides information to the media and public. Its website includes research reports, news reports, issue briefs, and more, including "Water Works: Rebuilding Infrastructure, Creating Jobs, and Greening the Government" and "Nine Reasons to Invest More in the Nation's Infrastructure."

Heritage Foundation

214 Massachusetts Ave. NE, Washington, DC   20002-4999
(202) 546-4400 • fax: (202) 546-8328
e-mail: info@heritage.org
website: www.heritage.org

The Heritage Foundation is a research and educational institute that promotes conservative public policies based on the principles of free enterprise, limited government, individual freedom, traditional American values, and a strong national defense. Its website includes numerous policy briefs, reports, and news items, including "The Limited Benefits of a National Infrastructure Bank" and "Obama vs. the Evidence: Infrastructure Spending Is No Job Creator."

Keston Institute for Public Finance and Infrastructure Policy

School of Policy, Planning, and Development
Marshall School of Business
University of Southern California
Ralph and Goldy Lewis Hall 232
Los Angeles, CA   90089-0626
(213) 740-4120 • fax: (213) 821-1039
website: www.usc.edu/schools/sppd/keston/index.php

The Keston Institute conducts research to further understanding and awareness of infrastructure challenges facing California and the nation. A central goal of the institute is to assist with policy decisions regarding public infrastructure development. Its website provides access to infrastructure research, including *Protecting the Public Interest: The Role of Long-Term Concession Agreements for Providing Transportation Infrastructure* and *Financing Civil Infrastructures: Is There a Role for Private Capital Markets?*

National Council for Public-Private Partnerships

2000 14th St. N, Suite 480, Arlington, VA   22201
(703) 469-2233 • fax: (703) 469-2236
website: http://ncppp.org

The National Council for Public-Private Partnerships is an organization of businesses and public officials interested in initiatives to provide public services. It advocates and facilitates the formation of public-private partnerships at the federal, state, and local levels, and raises the awareness of governments and businesses of the means by which their cooperation can effectively provide the public with quality goods, services, and facilities. On its website, the council publishes issue papers and speeches, including "Issues and Options for Increasing the Use of Tolling and Pricing to Finance Transportation Improvements."

US Department of Transportation (DOT)
1200 New Jersey Ave. SE, Washington, DC   20590
(202) 366-4000
website: www.dot.gov

The US Department of Transportation is a federal agency that oversees the US transportation system. Its website includes access to numerous reports, news items, press releases, speeches, and other publications. It also is the home of *Fast Lane*, the official blog of the US Secretary of Transportation.

Bibliography

Books

Seth Fletcher   *Bottled Lightning: Superbatteries, Electric Cars, and the New Lithium Economy.* New York: Hill and Wang, 2011.

Richard R. Geddes   *The Road to Renewal: Private Investment in U.S. Transportation Infrastructure.* Lanham, MD: Rowman & Littlefield Publishing Group, 2011.

Michael Grabell   *Money Well Spent?: The Truth Behind the Trillion-Dollar Stimulus, the Biggest Economic Recovery Plan in History.* New York: PublicAffairs, 2012.

Brian Hayes   *Infrastructure: A Field Guide to the Industrial Landscape.* New York: W.W. Norton & Company, 2005.

Wendell C. Lawther   *Privatizing Toll Roads: A Public-Private Partnership.* Westport, CT: Greenwood Publishing Group, 2000.

Barry B. LePatner   *Too Big to Fail: America's Failing Infrastructure.* Lebanon, NH: University Press of New England, 2010.

Matthys Levy and Richard Panchyk   *Engineering the City: How Infrastructure Works.* Chicago, IL: Chicago Review Press, 2000.

Catherine Lutz and Anne Lutz Fernandez

Carjacked: The Culture of the Automobile and Its Effect on Our Lives. Hampshire, UK: Palgrave Macmillan, 2010.

James McCommons and James Kunstler

Waiting on a Train: The Embattled Future of Passenger Rail Service—A Year Spent Riding Across America. White River Junction, VT: Chelsea Green, 2009.

Dan McNichol

The Roads That Built America: The Incredible Story of the U.S. Interstate System. New York: Sterling, 2005.

Jim Motavalli

High Voltage: The Fast Track to Plug in the Auto Industry. Emmaus, PA: Rodale Books, 2011.

Randal O'Toole

Gridlock: Why We're Stuck in Traffic and What to Do About It. Washington, DC: Cato Institute, 2009.

Don Peck

Pinched: How the Great Recession Has Narrowed Our Future and What We Can Do About It. New York: Crown Publishers, 2011.

Anthony Perl

New Departures: Rethinking Rail Passenger Policy in the Twenty-First Century. Lexington, KY: University Press of Kentucky, 2002.

| Christopher Steiner | *$20 Per Gallon: How the Inevitable Rise in the Price of Gasoline Will Change Our Lives for the Better.* New York: Grand Central Publishing, 2009. |

Periodicals and Internet Sources

| Michael Barone | "High-Speed Rail Doesn't Make Sense in China Either," American Enterprise Institute, February 20, 2011. www.aei.org. |

| John Cheves | "Crumbling Ohio River Bridges Highlight Nation's Aging Infrastructure," Kentucky.com, September 18, 2011. |

| *Economist* | "China's Infrastructure Splurge: Rushing on by Road, Rail, and Air," February 14, 2008. www.economist.com. |

| *Economist* | "Life in the Slow Lane," April 28, 2011. www.economist.com. |

| Chris Giblin | "Electric Car Infrastructure Coming to NYC," *City Limits*, July 27, 2010. www.citylimits.org. |

| Steve Hargreaves | "The Dam Infrastructure Problem," *CNNMoney*, April 9, 2009. www.money.cnn.com. |

| Barry B. LePatner, interviewed by Vivian Marino | "The 30-Minute Interview: Barry B. LePatner," *New York Times*, February 21, 2012. www.nytimes.com. |

Michael Lind	"Can Infrastructure-Led Growth Save the Economy?" *Salon*, July 13, 2010. www.salon.com.
Brad Plumer	"Is America's Infrastructure Really So Bad?" *Wonkblog—Washington Post*, November 1, 2011. www.washington post.com.
Ed Rendell	"Top Dem: Spend War Money on U.S. Infrastructure," *Salon*, December 7, 2010. www.salon.com.
Matt Sledge	"GOP Candidates' Transportation Infrastructure Talk Praises Tolls But Ignores Jobs," *Huffington Post*, January 4, 2012. www.huffingtonpost .com.
Erik Sofge and the Editors of Popular Mechanics	"The 10 Pieces of U.S. Infrastructure We Must Fix Now," *Popular Mechanics*, n.d. www.popular mechanics.com.
Laura D'Andrea Tyson	"The Infrastructure Twofer: Jobs Now and Future Growth," *Economix—New York Times*, October 21, 2011. http://economix.blogs .nytimes.com.
Ronald Utt	"Infrastructure Stimulus Spending: Pandering to Organized Labor," The Heritage Foundation, September 8, 2010. www.heritage.org.

Ronald Utt — "Obama's Peculiar Obsession with Infrastructure Banks Will Not Aid Economic Recovery," The Heritage Foundation, August 30, 2011. www.heritage.org.

Adam Vaughan — "Electric Car Infrastructure Begins to Roll Out Across the UK," *Environment Blog—Guardian*, October 14, 2011. www.guardian.co.uk/environment/blog.

Travis Waldron — "As America's Infrastructure Crumbles, GOP Presidential Candidates Refuse to Offer Solutions," Think Progress, January 3, 2012. http://thinkprogress.org.

Bryan Walsh — "Why Dropping the Gas Tax Would Be a Disaster," *Ecocentric—Time*, August 16, 2011. http://ecocentric.blogs.time.com.

Matthew Yglesias — "America's Infrastructure Cost Disaster," Think Progress, November 4, 2011. http://thinkprogress.org.

Matthew Yglesias — "America's Infrastructure Failure," *Moneybox—Slate*, December 30, 2011. www.slate.com.

Index